IDEAL HOME
Stylish BOOK OF Interiors

IDEAL HOME
Stylish BOOK OF Interiors

Janet Donin

BLANDFORD PRESS
POOLE · NEW YORK · SYDNEY

First published in the UK 1986 by Blandford Press
Link House, West Street, Poole, Dorset BH15 1LL

Text Copyright © 1986 Janet Donin

Illustrations copyright ©
Ideal Home magazine
and as credited

Distributed in the United States by
Sterling Publishing Co, Inc,
2 Park Avenue, New York, NY 10016

Distributed in Australia by
Capricorn Link (Australia) Pty Ltd
PO Box 665, Lane Cove, NSW 2066

British Library Cataloguing in Publication Data

Donin, Janet
  Ideal home book of stylish interiors.
  1. Interior decoration
  I. Title
  747′.022′2   NK2110

ISBN 0 7137 1856 0

Typeset by MS Filmsetting Ltd., Frome, Somerset

Printed in Great Britain by
Purnell Book Production Ltd., Paulton, Bristol

Contents

Foreword

THIS BOOK is a selection of the very best interiors taken from homes that have occupied pride of place in recent issues of *Ideal Home* magazine.

An ideal source of ideas and inspiration, the *Ideal Home Book of Stylish Interiors* covers an impressively comprehensive range of design styles and reflects a wide variety of taste.

I am sure that any reader interested in trends in interior decor or anyone seeking inspiration for their own home will find this book invaluable, providing as it does practical advice and a review of all the design and decorating choices available.

Finally, I would like to offer my personal thanks to Janet Donin for her dedication in producing this ultimate source of ideas in home decoration.

Terence Whelan
Editor, *Ideal Home* magazine

Introduction

I LOVE looking around other people's homes – don't you? It's not just being a voyeur, although homes are like autobiographies and tell you so much about the owner, but it's always fascinating to see how other people solve problems of space, storage and architectural quirks, as well as the way in which they furnish and decorate their homes. The only problem is that I'm usually so inspired by their achievements that I want to rush home and copy the ideas myself.

And that's really what this book is all about! It's a pictorial book of ideas, featuring over three hundred photographs of stylish interiors which have recently appeared in *Ideal Home* magazine. Interiors full of colourful, imaginative, tradtional, romantic and inspirational ideas, which you could interpret in your home.

Ideas which capture the imagination, like an interesting arrangement of prints, a collection of china or a display of musical instruments; creative ideas, like stencilled kitchen units or cupboards, canopied beds or beautifully curtained windows; and practical ideas, like boxed-in radiators, clever shelving and painting techniques. Not step-by-step instructions on how to copy them exactly, but ideas which hopefully will inspire you to create something similar yourself.

I also hope that this book will act as an incentive for you to think about your home more carefully. Yes, it is a place to relax in and be comfortable in, but it can also be as stylish as any of the interiors shown here. Don't be content with granny's old sofa or last year's sale bargain as a way to furnish your home: go out and browse around furniture showrooms and fabric shops for just the right chair or the perfect complementary fabric; nose in the far corners of antique markets for an unusual lamp or original door knob to add character to your home; and do plan each room carefully, matching colour samples of paint and fabric and even making sketches of shelving ideas or kitchen designs to avoid costly mistakes.

I began by saying how much I love to look around homes for inspiration, and by leafing through these pages I hope you too can be filled with the same inspiration and enthusiasm to create stylish interiors within your own home.

Janet Donin
1986

Architectural Review

HOUSES of character – Georgian, Edwardian, Victorian and even the 1930s semi – have so many inherent architectural features reflecting their style that it's a pity not to work with them rather than strip them away. Indeed, there are so many reproduction cornices, fireplaces and dado rails to be had that character can easily be replaced. In newer homes where ceilings are lower and walls straighter, character of a different kind can be achieved with wood-block flooring, original shelving and imaginative lighting. Individual details like a beautiful window or wooden beams and struts should be left perfectly plain, except perhaps for a spotlight, plant or picture carefully placed to accentuate the feature. Space problems are tricky, but think carefully before combining two reception rooms into one large area. Two rooms are often easier to furnish and to keep warm and their space could visually be doubled with clever use of mirrors. Rooms with lofty ceilings could be lowered with a canopy of fabric or a false ceiling. A raised floor area creating two levels could alter the feeling at ground level, or a balconied area could create more pleasing proportions. Style and arrangement of furniture is a matter of taste. Homes with a strong sense of character, whether traditional or modern, can look stunning with furniture that either reflects or contrasts with their style, but it is practically impossible to use heavy traditional furniture in a smaller home. However, one carefully chosen traditional chair or cabinet could say it all.

The rich, natural tones of this living room owe much to the restraint of its owners who have resisted the temptation to introduce contrasting colours, for nothing blends so well with natural brick as polished wood, soft leather and neutral-coloured soft furnishings.

Brickwork

Brickwork is one of those natural materials that happily spans the design barriers, as this living room illustrates. Against the background of red brick, which cleverly incorporates storage nooks and crannies, are the expansive shapes of leather Chesterfields and the elegance of a grand piano.

The hallway of this riverside home in Berkshire has walls and flooring of fair faced brick, and relies totally on shape and colour for its dynamic impression. In fact the circular stairwell, with its open-rise staircase, illustrates the versatility of rectangular brickwork.

When this artisan cottage was extended to resemble town house proportions, its character was in danger of slipping away. However, the introduction of a fireplace and chimney breast in old brick created the missing focal point. The interesting rustic quality cleverly complements the traditional furnishings.

Beam Ends

Creating two storeys from one, in this Suffolk retreat, meant using old timber for the support beams. Anything less weathered would have been totally out of character. As it is, these tough supports have created their own rustic style and blend well with old brick and polished wood furniture.

The central carved column of this ecclesiastical-style attic room gives the impression of supporting the structure. Of the same rich wood, the beams stretch out to support the roof and surround the window with such symmetry of style as to be very pleasing to the eye.

During the conversion of this unique country chapel, care was taken to incorporate all the inherent features wherever possible. In the main bedroom this curved beam, with its carved finial, softens the more rigid strut lines, to harmonise well with the pale colours and floral fabrics.

Clear Views

This spacious flat in the centre of Amsterdam overlooks one of the many canals. Small wonder, therefore, that its designer/owner decided to leave the beautiful curved windows unadorned, and let their lovely shapes speak for themselves rather than emphasising them with colour or curtains.

The window panels in this living room are stepped to follow the formation of the tiered ceiling. It's a distinctive feature that's carefully lit by an up-light on the side wall. The simple furnishings were also chosen in plain colours to prevent a clash of ideas and focal points.

Few homes can boast such a spectacular feature as this domed ceiling window, found on the upper landing of a Georgian house. It's an architectural detail that requires no adornment other than a single hanging plant, which serves to attract the eye to its existence.

New Dimensions

The balconied living-room-cum-bedroom of this artist's studio lets in all the light from a high north-facing window, without obstructing the view of works exhibited on the main studio wall. Turned wooden railings on both balcony and staircase help the feeling of space.

The impressive A-frame structure supporting the roof of this Cornish farmhouse is visible from many angles, since the owners decided on an intriguing open-plan interior. Rising from the living room, the central open-tread staircase meets the first-floor kitchen on one side and a simple dining room on the other.

Converted riverside warehouses make marvellous open-plan homes. Here the living, dining and kitchen areas take full advantage of the wall of windows. The timber-framed balcony to the bedrooms carefully edges the windows and blends well with the ever-changing view beyond the windows.

Whitewashed

Natural building materials can be painted white to bridge the gap between modern and traditional surroundings. Here the contemporary white painted brickwork marries the timbered floor and ceiling to the traditional soft furnishings of the living room.

The joining of the two rooms in this Victorian house has been accomplished with architectural ease. The white painting of the wall and ceiling surfaces has camouflaged any differences in the picture rail mouldings, skirting boards and ceiling struts, while the clever positioning of the neutral-coloured sofa also helps the deception.

Opposite: The Gothic-style windows of this Buckinghamshire house would have been at odds with the heavily-beamed ceiling, had not the owners painted both architectural details in white. Clever use of neutral tones for the soft furnishings also helps to span the style barriers.

Country House

ALL THOSE childhood images of country cottages with rough-cast walls, timbered furniture and wild flowers still hold true for the country house today. Perhaps it is not quite so romantic, thanks to central heating backing up the open log fire, but essentially the simplicity is the same. Pine furniture topped with floral cloths or cushions, bare floorboards or quarry tiles softened with rag rugs or colourful dhurries, and flowery furnishings everywhere. The true country house is also full of collected paraphernalia, for just like the country mouse its owner stores and hordes everything: dried flowers hanging from wooden beams; wicker baskets filled with everything from magazines to make-up; gleaming copper or brass; scraps of lace and patchwork, and the inevitable pots of preserves. The atmosphere is very special too; there's a smell of beeswax in the air from the constant polishing of wood, colours are soft and mellow like the petals in a bowl of pot pourri and there's the kind of tranquillity that is only to be found in casual, comfortable interiors. However, this style and atmosphere don't rely on country lanes and villages alone for they can be equally at home in suburbia, if you make it so!

Flowers are essential to the country house style and in this sunny bedroom they are everywhere, thanks to the co-ordinating range of linen and furnishings by Dorma. Mellow pine floorboards complement the look, but be careful not to overdo the stripped pine feeling. Here the wooden ceiling and lower walls have been painted white for a softer country look.

Floral Tribute

Reminiscent of a country garden, this Sanderson wallpaper and matching fabric is strewn with poppies, tulips and primulas and creates a floral bower within the room. The wooden panelling and beams are picked out in a complementary green colour which allows for a generous helping of pine furniture. The effect is pleasantly cluttered without being overpowering.

A warm airy kitchen is one of the best places to dry flowers, which can become part of a pervading country atmosphere. Cornflowers, hydrangeas, stocks, carnations, roses and delphinium flowers all dry well when tied in small bunches and hung upside down from the ceiling.

Opposite: Country house, American-style, is the nature of this living room where the flowers are bolder and brighter. A neat touch is the fabric edging to the Terylene blinds. The breath of country air, however, rests truly with the delightful pine love seat.

Preferably Pine

Rescued from a church demolition site, these cut-down pine pews with their sleek mahogany trim fit neatly into the breakfast nook of a country kitchen. The refectory-style pine table was also fashioned to fit. And with patchwork cushions on the seat and dried flowers on the table the country look couldn't be more complete.

The pine kitchen cupboards of this Victorian house in Lancashire are actually made from new wood, but the owner cleverly stained them to look more mature. Matched with the rough-cast walls, terracotta flooring and traditional accessories they blend well with the style of the house.

Opposite: The beauty of pine furniture is that no matter what its age it always looks attractive. Reproduction furniture made from old pine, like this, however, is obviously in better condition. Generous helpings of beeswax enrich the patina, and with age even new pine improves.

Rustic Charm

This converted kitchen in a Cheshire family house has all the qualities of rustic charm, yet the materials are new. Bricks form the basis of all the units, though their mortar has been channelled out to give an aged appearance; the matching quarry tiles on floor and worktops have a rich russet tone, while all the new pine is gradually mellowing with age.

The dining room of this country cottage, on the borders of Suffolk, dates back to the seventeenth century. Now the plain wattle-and-daub construction, interlaced with supporting beams, is painted Suffolk pink and marries well with the traditional oak furniture and quarry-tiled floor.

Opposite: The making of corn dollies is a traditional country craft, though in this sunny setting their rustic quality serves only to emphasise the freshness of the cowslip-coloured walls, in Dulux paint, and the flower-sprigged café curtains. The patchwork and painted cushions on the chair are also traditional crafts.

Country Grand

Transporting the furnishings of a town house to a country retreat can sometimes be disastrous, but the burnished tones of these comfortable sofas and walnut coffee table harmonise well with the timbered ceiling and wall struts of this East Anglian country home.

Larger country homes often have bedrooms whose proportions almost demand the inclusion of a traditional four-poster bed. This one made of chestnut wood by Smallbone has a tapestry-style bedspread and canopy to add to the feeling of grandeur, but nothing could be more evocative than the bedroom fire.

The polished baby grand takes pride of place in the living room of what is actually a small town house. But there's no denying the feeling of country grandeur with the quarry-tile flooring nudging the antique writing desk and the pervading atmosphere of organised clutter.

Rural Qualities

Townies can emulate their country cousins with a few traditional touches like the pine wall cabinet, bentwood chairs and gingham cloth. This doesn't mean that they have to sacrifice the typically town house touches of floor-sweeping curtains or a matched set of posters.

No matter what the location, a brick fireplace with combined log storage area and display shelves will inevitably have a rural quality. In this living room its charm is emphasised by the painted brick wall and the flower-sprigged curtains.

With the cooker set into a brick chimney breast, copper pans hanging from a beamed ceiling and a delightful conservatory beyond, this kitchen in a large suburban house couldn't look more rural; a quality which is helped by the marked lack of matched units.

City Looks

FOR MANY, this style of interior is very easy to live with. Based on tradition, it's a mélange of tastes which can be adapted to a variety of house types. Character is important, which means putting back, or even introducing, architectural details like dado rails, cornices and traditional fireplaces. Colours can be soft and co-ordinated or rich and smooth, but they must blend together rather than contrast, for there should be nothing here to jangle the nerves. Hard furniture should be mahogany or maple, never pine; or perhaps painted in ivory and given one of the revived decorating treatments of dragging or stippling. Soft furniture is just that, sumptuous and comfortable. Curtains are always floor-length and very full, plumped up with interlining and caught in elaborate tie-backs. Festoon blinds also complement the look, especially in bedrooms, but they must also be lined. 'City looks' is a style of interior for people who live ordered lives, keep diaries and entertain frequently, and where dogs and children have their proper place. A style that needs pampering with ever-increasing collections of pretty cushions, silver-framed photographs and endless vases of fresh flowers. In fact it's an inspirational style that can probably find a home in at least one room of any house, anywhere.

True city traditionalists delight in rescuing and restoring old furniture, which is just what fabric and wallpaper producers Cindy and Philip Edwards did with the comfortable sofas and pair of matching chairs in their living room. Exquisite fabrics are essential to the idea, and a generous smattering of old mahogany furniture, to offset the pale colour scheme, is an important luxury touch.

Richly Traditional

All that was left of the character in this Edwardian town house was the cornice and fireplace, but clever use of wallpapers and borders produced a style of decorating reminiscent of the era. The new dado rail is edged with a narrow border and matched with a wider replica below the cornice. Co-ordinating wallpapers pattern the walls, while the curtain fabric incorporates all the patterns and provides a rich background to the elegant dining table and chairs.

Although essentially pale, this elegant drawing room has a richness of colour that stems from the deep Art Nouveau frieze surrounding the walls at ceiling height. From this, the turquoise and coral accented theme was taken and reproduced in the elegantly pelmeted curtains and traditionally covered furniture.

Opposite: Richly-patterned wallpapers and fabrics, like these by Laura Ashley, create a strength of character that's vital to city traditionalists. Old mahogany furniture nudging tasselled footstools, leather-bound books and cases and the inevitable riding boots, all in shades of burgundy, brown and ochre, produce an atmosphere that's steeped in heritage and tradition.

Perfect Panelling

Regency homes were distinctive for their beautifully panelled rooms, which is why the owners of this elegant house in Bath went to great lengths to interpret the style in their home. The beaded panels are painted white, while two shades of soft yellow are used to decorate the walls.

Fitted wardrobes have absolutely no character of their own, but panelled with neat beading and painted in contrasting colours they can add an important traditional note to any style of home. Antique accessories help the deception and a generous use of fabric in curtains and table cloths promotes a feeling of luxury. Subtle, harmonising colours also create a restful atmosphere.

Opposite: A quiet corner of this elegant town house was used to promote the owners' love of wood panelling. Following the proportions of the tall shutters, the same panels were used to back the fake alcove which has been cleverly lit to highlight an arrangement of glass and silverware.

Reflected Style

Epitomising the city classic style this living room is rich with pattern and architectural details, yet the restrained colour scheme is restful and luxurious. For these very reasons the large mirrors either side of the fireplace work wonders, doubling the size of the room without reflecting disturbing images. Note the gathered fabric behind the cupboard doors, the framing round the mirrors and the boxed-in radiators.

Built in the 1950s, this house has adapted well to the notion of 'city looks', with its pale grey walls and carpet, and toning yellow checked fabric and painted furniture. The effect is soft and luxurious and all is reflected in a large mirror which spans one wall.

Long, narrow drawing rooms created by combining two reception areas can achieve more pleasing proportions by introducing a complete wall of mirror. In this elegant London home, mirrors are placed behind the glass shelves that flank the fireplace, and also on the chimney breast.

Pale Classics

Mahogany is one of those richly-coloured woods that looks superb with pale tones, and is a favourite combination for city homes. Marrying the various colours is lovely linen by Dorma which introduces an apricot shade to this bedroom; this is also picked up by the dhurries on the painted wooden floor.

Lofty attic rooms need the palest of colour schemes to prevent feelings of claustrophobia. Here the background colour of pale apricot also covers the fitted cupboards under the window. Summer blue complements the shade beautifully, and not only covers the bed but is cleverly picked out as a detail on the cupboards and lamp bases.

The pale green and cream colour scheme, in the bedroom of this London *pied-à-terre*, gives the most relaxing of shades for a small room. The tonal quality of the colours is also identical, which is why the combination is so appealing. The oriental wall-hanging above the bed echoes the softness of the colours.

Mirrored Elegance

Few overmantel mirrors are so ornately gilded and patterned as this, which because of the lofty proportions of the room and the embellishment on the marble fireplace looks perfectly at home. Wisely, the owner of this London flat has chosen not to decorate the pale pink walls in any other way and allows the elegant mirror to stand alone.

In this Victorian terraced cottage, the limited light in the open plan ground floor area is expansively reflected by a wide mirror. This was cleverly created by framing ordinary mirror plate with deep picture moulding. The wood was then stained to match the mellow pine of the dresser below.

Opposite: The best place for a mirror is in a position where it can not only look elegant but where it can also practically reflect light or limited space. Happily, this curved mirror does both, located as it is above a console table, where it echoes the shape of the garden door and reflects the available light.

Special Effects

PAINTING to achieve special effects is not a new art form. In the Georgian era, decorators used special glazes to create varied effects, and the Romans were gifted in the art of mural painting. However, the recent revival of traditional decorating techniques has created a renewed interest in the embellishment of our homes. Rag-rolling, sponge-painting, dragging and marbling are all skilled crafts, but if you approach the task with a sense of fun it is possible to achieve some interesting amateur results. For the less than skilled, eggshell or emulsion paints are ideal and their various applications using dry cloths, sea sponges, clean brushes or feathers relies totally on the requirements of the individual. However, you really need to be artistic to create a mural, but the price of a professional may be well within your reach if you want something really special. Effects with wallpapers and borders are of course the easiest to achieve, and with so many co-ordinated ranges to choose from the permutations are endless. Borders outlining windows and doors, or edging dado rails and skirting boards, create new and varied dimensions to a room; and for an instant injection of character the many mock covings, dado rails and beadings can introduce all kinds of special effects.

Uniquely clever borders have been created by Interior Selection to co-ordinate with their mosaic range of wallpapers and fabrics. Their variation lies with a pattern that diffuses out of the background, into a linear highlight. Here the border is used with its matching wallpaper to create panels on a wall and define the edges of a low table.

Border Lines

Probably the easiest way to inject colour and pattern into a room without completely redecorating it is with a border. Bought by the metre it is easy to apply, but you must mitre the corners. Use it at ceiling height in a lofty room but at a lower level in smaller areas. In this bathroom a border is used to divide the pretty from the practical elements.

A tiny window with an uninspiring view gets the full treatment. This distinctive border with mitred corners surrounds the window frame to give it more definition, while its colours are echoed in the pretty tapestry pictures on either side. The Jacquard lacy Terylene net is gathered into soft café curtains to camouflage the uninteresting view and complete the picture.

Victorian houses like this one in Sussex often have their bedroom fireplaces intact. Since they are usually quite small, a pretty border can draw attention to their existence and emphasise their character. This one in pink and white, matched with pink accessories, is particularly attractive.

Cupboard and Drawer Effects

Stencilled furniture is all the more effective if its colours and pattern echo those of a fabric. Collier Campbell's 'Romany' fabric with its stylish cabbage rose pattern was a natural choice in this bedroom. Cut your own stencils by tracing the pattern from the fabric, then interpret it on stencil paper.

Wooden units, even in a kitchen, are prime targets for special effects, and at this country home in Suffolk they look remarkably in character. The units, designed by Smallbone, have been hand-dragged in blue paint over white eggshell, then stencilled on both cupboard doors and drawers. Two coats of clear varnish protect the effect and give them a practical finish.

A neat arrangement of cupboard doors and drawers tucked into a stairwell has been given a unique treatment by Dragons. The painted door panels reflect the contents of the cupboards, while the sliding drawers beneath were perfect for stylised car fronts.

Magical Murals

Alison Bauld is an original artist and musician, whose talents come together in a fantasy mural in the bedroom of her London home. Reflecting the checked bedspread and striped curtains, the wall of cupboard doors maintains the black and white theme and incorporates both piano and artist's model.

When the view from your window is rooftops and office blocks, an imaginary glimpse of a spring garden is most welcome. Artist Peter Payne created this 'room with a view' on a wall and cupboard door of a city flat. Making it all the more real are the snoozing cat and discarded running shoes.

Opposite: Artist Tim Plant created this wondrous, room-enveloping mural in the dining room of an Italian villa. Its effect is to bring the surrounding countryside within the room. The trompe-l'oeil view through the window, which was in fact painted on a blank wall, encourages the eye to view imaginary vistas.

Decorative Treatments

Several special effects come together in this elegant room. The walls were sponge-painted in two shades of yellow, the cupboard doors were dragged in the same shades, while the coffee table was rag-rolled to match. Dulux Matchmaker paints in vinyl silk and silthane finishes were used throughout, which is encouragement indeed for the amateur decorator to try his hand.

The beauty of sponge-painting, as designer Marlène Acock shows here, is that any tired piece of furniture can be given a new lease of life. This bedside table, once a dirty cream colour, was sponge-painted in three shades of blue, plus a smattering of gold, to create this unique effect.

Marble-painting is a skilled craft, but in the hands of an amateur original effects can still be created. The stylised fireplace in this room has been marble-painted in three shades of Dulux silthane silk paints and, though not strictly resembling the real thing, it is nevertheless very eye-catching.

Paint Details

Busy patterns can be overpowering in new homes, while neutral shades may be too bland. A blending of the two ideas therefore can create some interesting special effects. Here the walls were angled with masking tape and then defined in a deep shade of coral paint. When dry, a pale blue paint was applied on top, using a patterned roller.

The plain canvas of blank walls in a modern apartment is ripe for special effects. In this study a mock dado rail has been introduced between shocking pink rag-rolled areas and plain white walls. The effect is stunning and cleverly incorporates a plain door into the scheme of things.

Neutral colour schemes are pleasant and relaxing but a bold statement with colour can prevent them from becoming boring, especially in a modern home. Inspiration strikes on a short wall painted in clear turquoise which is followed through on the coving of the adjacent walls. Intriguing stripes around the corner are in the same colour and are made possible by extensive use of masking tape.

Colour Confidence

N SPITE of what the pundits may say, decorating with colour is really a matter of confidence and individual choice, but a quick glance at the colour wheel will help you to avoid mistakes. Of course it makes sense to choose warm shades for a cold north-facing room and cool tones for a bright south-facing room, but the choice is yours. Basically you can choose from three forms of colour interpretation. If you lack colour confidence the easiest solution is to choose a single colour theme for a room, but this in itself can incorporate many shades of a colour like primrose, lemon, sunflower, saffron, mustard and ochre. Alternatively, you could choose a toning scheme made up of those colours which lie closest in the colour wheel, like indigo, mid-blue, turquoise and pale green. Contrasting colour schemes are the most difficult to get right for they use colours from opposite sides of the wheel, like red with green or blue with orange, but if you soften the tones to, say, red with pastel green or olive, or mid-blue with sand, you could have the basis of a successful scheme that will not lose favour.

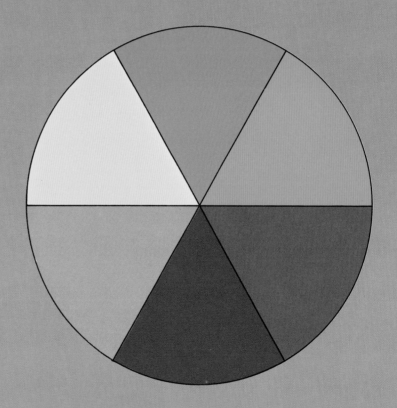

Yellow is one of those marvellous colours that brings sunshine to any room. It works particularly well in this room because the colour is concentrated on the walls and on the furniture positioned against them, while the rest of the room is decorated and furnished in neutral tones. However, in this room it was important to keep all the shades of yellow identical.

Creative Mix

The contrasting colour scheme of bright red and blue is held together, in this children's bathroom, by the neutral grey tones of the walls, floor and work surfaces. The varied linear effects of the Runtalrad column radiator, Venetian blind and painted surrounds add to the dramatic effect.

It's surprising how a stunning monochrome scheme of white walls with black floor and furniture can suddenly take on new dimensions with a boldly-coloured rug. The only other concession to colour in the room is the deep green paintwork and red tulips. To change the whole effect, all that's necessary is a new rug.

Colour in this combined living and dining room is concentrated at floor level where the clear green and blue of the sofa perfectly match the carpet and dividing wall. Bright yellow in the dining room is set against shiny black and the whole area is surrounded by neutral white walls.

Primary School

A small study or tiny living room becomes instantly dramatic with a hot red colour scheme. However, it is important that all the reds of both paint and fabric should be identical, like these by Laura Ashley. Contrasting colours would be too strong in this room, so all the accessories are in shades of brown, black and brass.

Living with a single colour in a small space can have an enveloping, comforting effect. The success of this bright yellow dining room relies on the complete matching of the yellow on walls and furniture, with the light relief of a white floor and limited green accessories.

Evoking images of sun and sand, this small office has the solid mass of clear blue broken by linear stripes in soft yellow. Injecting a jokey atmosphere to the room are the tall palm and sun-like lamp. Once again the neutral floor and furniture balance the scheme.

Colour Plan

Planned colour is a way of creating a focal point in a room. Here the overall theme is neutral, but the centre of attention is this colourful sofa. Because it is so eye-catching it makes a positive colour statement without being overpowering and allows scope to use the same colours as accessories throughout the room.

Clever colour planning can mean using shades from opposite ends of the spectrum, which have a certain continuity because their tonal quality is the same. The leaf green and apple blossom pink scheme in this bedroom takes its colour key from nature, with the result that it is restful yet colourful.

Opposite: Based on a simple red and white theme, the colour plan of this bathroom intrinsically involves a pattern plan as well. The colourful horizontal bands of tiles are all planned to coincide with the specific levels of the floor, bidet, wash basin, mirror and ceiling.

Bold Statements

At first glance this room may look full of contrasting colours, but basically it is a bold black and white scheme, sparked with a generous dollop of red and a smattering of blue and yellow. Of course pattern plays a strong part, but the solid blocks of colour prevent the room from losing its continuity.

Red and yellow are a pair of hot colours which can make a dramatic impact, especially in a small room like this bedsitter. Potentially gloomy, with just one small window, it relies totally on colour and clever lighting to give it warmth and intimacy. To prevent overcrowding, it is also important to avoid too many other shades.

Opposite: The most dramatic colour of all is black, which as a wallcovering is often difficult to use successfully. However, in this small attic bathroom, with the walls painted in Cover Plus black matt vinyl, it could not look more stunning. White fittings, a colourful print and plenty of natural foliage prevent the scheme from looking too flat, but the most important feature is the wide window providing shafts of natural light.

Relative Shades

Blue can be either a warm or cool colour, depending on its partiality for green or violet undertones. Here the periwinkle blue of the wall has a warm tendency, which is emphasised by the use of red accessories. So, although the two colours contrast, they do have similar undertones.

Of all contrasting colours, yellow and blue, so synonymous with sun and sky, have a particular affinity. In this room where the colour has a definite place – yellow on the walls, blue in the furniture and neutral beige on the floor – it works particularly well.

Opposite: Blue, green and yellow lie next to one another in the colour wheel and can create particularly restful colour schemes if their tonal quality is tinged with black, to give this a mellow appearance. Here the blue and yellow wallpaper blends well with the natural wood fireplace and complements the dull green sofa.

Designer Touches

INTERIOR designers may set the fashion trends in colour and style but the basis of their craft relies on those important little touches that separate them from the amateur decorator. Here are some tricks of the trade: besides lining material, always use interlining for a full, extravagant look in curtains; drape them with interesting tie-backs like heavy chandler's cord, or a plait of three fabric tubes lightly filled with wadding; and always use a deep heading unless there is a proper pelmet. Be generous with fabrics of soft, sophisticated effects; have extra-long curtains and floor-length table cloths that tumble to the floor; gathered fabric panels fixed within cupboard doors instead of wooden panels; an exquisite silk shawl or cashmere travelling rug slung across the back of a sofa and tiers of crisp lace over beds. Surround book shelves with deep wooden mouldings or fake hardboard arches; box in radiators with panelair or wooden trellis; add beading to make panels on cupboard doors and to edge work surfaces. Always have one antique piece of furniture within any room, no matter what its style: a Victorian chair, an inlaid writing desk, a butler's table or a Persian rug can create instant character. Lighting must always be diffused, created by table lamps, soft up-lights or picture lights, instead of just a single overhead light; and experiment with dimmer switches. Beautifully-framed pictures displayed in groups, and large-framed mirrors to create extra dimensions and interesting reflections of light, are important. Finally, if you are less than skilled in any craft, always employ a professional, who with a bit of luck will make even the cheapest materials look expensive!

Radiators are rather ugly, if essential, features of a home, which is why designers like to camouflage them with attractive casings. Here the trellis-style front allows the heat to circulate through the hall, and with a useful shelf above transforms the radiator area into a much more attractive necessity

Cupboard Love

Designer Janie Sinclair fell in love with some grey limed wood she had seen in Australia and, with the image firmly imprinted on her mind, tried to achieve the same effect on her bedroom cupboards. The result is soft and subtle in shades of white, beige and grey. The exquisite fabric-painted headboard is her own work and blends well with the country feel of the room.

Thanks to people like Smallbone, hand-painted kitchens like this one are changing the face of the old cookhouse. The cupboard doors were painted to match the walls, then marbled with green paint. All the work surfaces are cream-coloured Corian and the special decoration is the poppy-painted wall and floor.

Opposite: Classically elegant, this drawing room features several designer tricks, from the plain curtains with their patterned edging panel and plaited tie-backs, to the wallpaper border defining the curved alcove and fireplace, and the shaped cupboards with their moulded detailing and pleated fabric panels. Here the wallpapers and fabrics are by designer Sue Stowell.

Fabrication

High-ceilinged bedrooms show off canopied beds to perfection. Here the bed has a half tester canopy with pleated frill and matching curtain. Roman blinds are used at the windows, to avoid distraction from the bed, and the Smallbone fitted units are all painted in complementary colours.

Windows invariably come in for designer treatment, and with tall windows like these, in the home of wallpaper and fabric producer Philip Edwards, it's the pelmet that is special. Undulating around the window it matches the curtains but has a pencil pleat heading and a narrow, gathered frill on the bottom edge in a contrasting colour.

Camouflaged furniture shrouded in pretty fabric and softened with armloads of cushions can change the whole feel of a tired room. Here the fabric, by Collier Campbell, is in a variety of abstract designs which blend well with the traditional desk, country pots and jokey tied-up coffee tables.

Space Stories

The repetitive outline of the blind and banner treated window, which is reflected in the shape of the display shelves, acts like a mirror reflection and confuses the eye into imagining more space than actually exists. Of course the neutral colour scheme also helps.

Dividing an elegant room, with its ornate coving, into a practical kitchen and dining room was cleverly achieved by designer Doreen Bond, who has not compromised the wonderful feeling of space. A low partition now divides the two areas, and is decorated with fake panels to preserve the traditional feel.

Converting a large bedroom into a second bathroom can often produce too much space, but here the problem has been solved by a small platform at one end of the bath, which can be used as a neat dressing area. The white and gold colour scheme and the toning panelling on the Poggenpohl units adds that extra touch of luxury.

On Reflection

Designers love walls of mirrors, especially in narrow rooms where they can effectively double the space. Large mirror plate, though, can be impractical as well as expensive. In this bathroom mirror tiles achieve the same effect. The extra designer touch is the tiny strip of colour co-ordinated beading on the top and bottom edges.

A perfect use of mirrors has been incorporated into this narrow dressing area and adjacent bathroom. A large mirror set with overhead lights lines the alcove behind the washbasin. Mirror is also used on the wall behind the toilet to reflect all the light and space in the room.

A beautifully-framed mirror looks very elegant in a hall and can reflect the limited light, which is often a problem in halls. Here the original console table has also been inlaid with mirror for the same reason. Be careful to edge mirrors at floor level with a wooden kickboard to prevent breaking.

Colour Trends

Pioneer of fashion trends in furnishings, designer Tricia Guild has created this range of wallpapers and fabrics for Next. Although we have always thought of her in connection with pastel shades, this deep terracotta combination has all the hallmarks of design success.

Darker colours are the current design favourites, but they should be used with an element of caution in small town houses and apartments. Here the deep purple is concentrated on the sofas, but the cleverly co-ordinating rug and deep yellow accessories all lighten the room.

The battleship grey, painted on the walls of this study, looked very gloomy before designer Judy Elliott introduced the glowing cerise colour of the easy chair cover. However, the room loses none of its masculinity or continuity, especially with the grey and cerise striped Roman blinds at the windows.

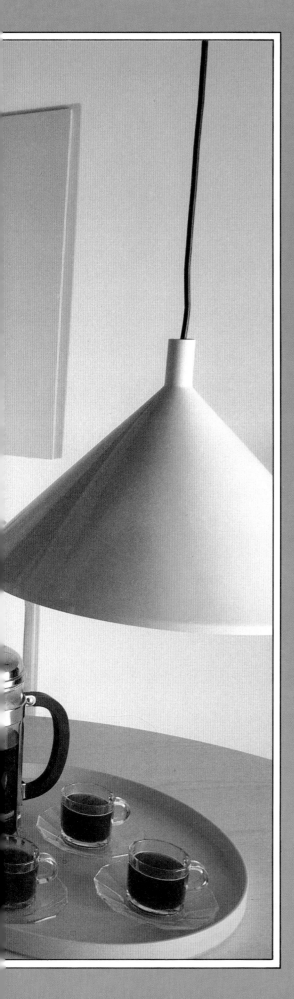

Inspirational

PURE GENIUS may be a bit of an exaggeration, but sometimes decorative inspiration strikes in such a curious way that you just can't believe it! Misty memories of a particular painting or movie set, or an article you have seen in a magazine, might suddenly be remembered and inspire you to create something original; like grouping a collection of old violins in a fireplace grate, or papering a screen with photographs and cuttings as the Victorians did, or edging a new white blind with old lace to give it character. Ideas with fabric can be more extensive, like looping great lengths over suspended rods to form a bed canopy, or sewing sheeting material to resemble curtains, then fixing it on battens around a tiny bedroom to form a camouflaging wall covering, or simply draping an exotic silk shawl over a shabby armchair. Inspirational shelving around windows and doors, or under stairs and above beds, can solve storage problems, while screens made from garden trellis, Venetian blinds or even radiators can be great space makers. The origination of new ideas is as plentiful and exciting as your imagination, but here are a few more to inspire you.

Inspired and infinitely effective works of art can be as simple as this. The yellow, orange and blue squares were actually cut from a single sheet of chipboard, with the outline of the squares scored into the board. The shapes were then painted to match the various accessories in what is otherwise a very plain room.

Decorative Details

Not so much a question of using up the leftovers but more an inspired use of complementary wallpapers, this chequerboard wall is ideal for anyone seeking effect and with plenty of time to achieve it. Essential to the success of the scheme is to mark up the wall carefully and trim the paper neatly before you start decorating.

High drama in a hallway creates immediate impact. Inspiring this setting was the shape of the unusual chair which is echoed on the wall patterning. This was achieved by overlaying triangular wallpaper shapes onto a plain blue background. The choice of colours was influenced by the picture on the wall.

When this bathroom and separate loo were converted into one room, a small window became superfluous to the overall scheme of things. What better use of the window framing, therefore, than to use one of the children's delightful drawings, mounted on hardboard, to fill the space?

Screen Play

Large bedrooms can often use their space more effectively by simple division. At the foot of the bed an open screen of square trellis, to the exact width of the bed, divides the sleeping area from the dressing-room-cum-breakfast area. It is an inspired trick that makes two rooms of one without blocking any available light.

Clever decorating ideas turn this traditional room into something much more modern. Plain oak flooring is the basis. At the windows contemporary blinds match the fireplace screen. Deep blue paints the table bases, skirting board and coving, while creating an effective screen to divide a small office area are four square pillars.

Radiators were never like this before, but the designers who created Runtalrad column and panel radiators had our homes very much in mind. Painted yellow, the column radiator divides the kitchen and dining areas, while the panel radiator backs up against the wall, looking much more like a colourful work of art.

Artful Display

Industrial shelving and storage trays are extremely practical in this unique galley style kitchen. Painted green, the shelves match the studded green rubber on the walls and work surfaces, while the storage trays and taps are in yellow. Butcher's hooks clip onto the shelves to hold brushes, knives and scissors.

You either love or hate open shelves in a kitchen but at least you can see the contents of the jars! Pine and red co-ordinates this open shelf kitchen and across the window is a pine curtain rail hung with much used utensils on ordinary butcher's hooks.

Opposite: Nobody ever really makes use of the hall as a room, but here a narrow shelving unit holds an overflow of books, acts as a hall table and also camouflages the radiator in one simple natural wood unit. Another smaller unit is tucked into the corner of the hall, at its junction with the dining room.

High Drama

In the spotlight any room can be dramatic, and if the colour scheme fits the situation even more so. Here black, grey and white is the monochrome scheme, but with the precise lighting of a double wall spot and standard spot the room takes on an extra shimmer. Catching the light are the carefully-positioned dried flowers and arrangement of fruit.

Snatching inspiration from foreign lands is an instant design trick. Here the rich black and white linen by Dorma, the ruddy hue of rosewood and flickers of red, combine to create an exotic bedroom worthy of an eastern sunset.

Opposite: An abundance of fabric in rich colours and patterns can create instant drama. Collier Campbell design some of the most richly dramatic fabrics and in this setting you can see the effect of pattern on pattern. In a small alcove the same effect is possible even if you use a mixture of wallpaper, paint and fabric.

Level Best

Inspiration of an architectural nature is particularly applaudable, such as this neat pine kitchen which tucks under a stairwell. The clever marrying of pine from the staircase to the kitchen gives credibility to the scheme and the continuous flow of stripped floorboards in all areas creates an important continuity.

Creating space in what is actually a tiny cottage requires more than a smattering of inspiration. Here the second bedroom soars to an elevated platform above a series of cupboards on a wide landing below. A cautionary note is struck by the encircling metal banister.

Opposite: Bunk beds take on many different forms, but there can be none quite so dramatic as this elevated sleeping quarter, with its high-level, built-in sound system. Industrial scaffolding creates the structure, but dramatic colouring is responsible for the soporific mood.

Eclectic Display

ECLECTIC magpies are a breed apart. Incorrigible hoarders, they will collect anything and everything, before finally settling with their one true love. Collectors of Carlton Ware china, Clarice Cliff pottery and old prints have depleted the market and raised the prices, as have the devotees of Art Deco and Art Nouveau paraphernalia. But, if you are a novice in the eclectic art, don't be deterred, as the supplies are not yet exhausted. There are still model cars, cute little pigs and decoy ducks to be bagged. And, for the more avant garde, consider violins, napkin holders, snuff boxes and 'bad taste' flying birds. Impulsive collectors, however, must beware, for their eclectic natures could result in a rather ugly museum home rather than an amusing, tongue-in-cheek approach to design. Display, of course, is the key to organised clutter and the acceptable face of eclectic design. Pictures must be planned in their ultimate positions before hanging, to avoid an ugly carelessness. Model cars, pigs and thimbles should be tucked away on structured shelves. The only casual arrangements of collections that really work are those in such numbers that their sheer abundance is a decorative feature. However, remember that one cow on its own could look juvenile, while a complete herd makes a statement.

When a variety of pictures and prints are clustered together, it does not really matter whether their shapes, frames or subject matter are related. In this room they are arranged around two wall lights, filling the space between the heavy doors with interest.

Picturesque

A number of tiny prints displayed on a large wall must be in a tight arrangement to avoid looking lost. This display of water colours, medals, cartoons and miniature portraits was carefully stage-managed on the floor before a picture hook went into the wall. Even the perimeters of the display were marked on the wall first.

Sepia photographs of relatives, or even non-relatives, create marvellously nostalgic corners. These look particularly attractive because of their lovely Victorian frames. The haphazard arrangement is also pleasing and suggests that the collection will be added to.

Opposite: The dominant ancestral portrait on this wall of pictures makes a positive colour link with the black leather Chesterfield, and holds this formal arrangement of pictures and furniture together. Even the frames of the surrounding prints have been chosen to complement the more ornate frame of the central portrait and the brass lamp bases.

Mixed Blessings

Arranging a variety of pictures and memorabilia on a wall, in conjunction with more treasures on a table below, is slightly more tricky. Here the plant on the pine washstand fills the gap left by the pictures, while the dried flowers on the wall marry with the jug of grasses on the floor.

Light and space are the keynotes to this dramatic, if formal, arrangement. Every item can be enjoyed individually, and also as a whole. The contrast between the soft silk flowers and the straight picture frames, and between the little Victorian light and the chair back, is particularly pleasing.

Individual groups of eclectic treasures can be enjoyed within one room, providing the background colours do not fight for attention. Here the bone china on the dresser complements the ornate chest, while the more rustic clock and keys marry with the wooden chairs.

Shelf Contained

Lots of little pigs could clutter up many a windowledge or table if displayed individually, and their curious comparability would be lost. This large custom-made shelving unit with its moulded edge, however, creates much more impact.

The practicalities of storing collections of small items usually determine their display. A large collection of metal cars and buses, such as this, would be lost on a table, but arranged in display boxes they can be truly appreciated – and there will be no problems of dust or damage.

Curiously this sixties-style chrome and glass display unit creates a remarkable foil for a wondrous collection of Art Deco figures, Victorian glass and Art Nouveau photo frames. As the material elements are comparable, the drama of the display is even more effective.

Curious Collections

Even if you do not play a musical instrument, their decorative value to a collector can be equally valid. This sextet is grouped in a pleasing arrangement and becomes much more credible when married, as it is, to the music stand.

A row of painted clock faces is visually as pleasing as any picture, but their curiosity value is of more interest. Although similar in shape, each is individually patterned and the numerals vary from Roman to Arabic.

The twenties and thirties were a rich era for design in anything from luscious figures to enamelled boxes and vases. It was also a dramatic period, for the colours were invariably monochromed or murky. This small arrangement is typical of the style and makes a positive statement in its own right.

Collective Enterprise

Collecting china is one of the most popular pastimes, and although the cost of pretty pink and green Carlton Ware or more dramatic Clarice Cliff china has rapidly increased they still make worthwhile acquisitions. This beautiful oak dresser is the perfect display area for such collections.

This collection of jugs is particularly pleasing because, although cleverly co-ordinated to complement the bathroom's colour scheme, their handles are very individual, varying from a parrot to a hunter, a fox's tail to a palm tree.

China cows make a curious collection and, while the herd is still relatively small, it looks at home on top of this ornate chest of drawers. However, collections such as these are very precious and do not welcome excessive handling, so as the collection grows they will be put out to pasture in a glass-fronted cabinet.

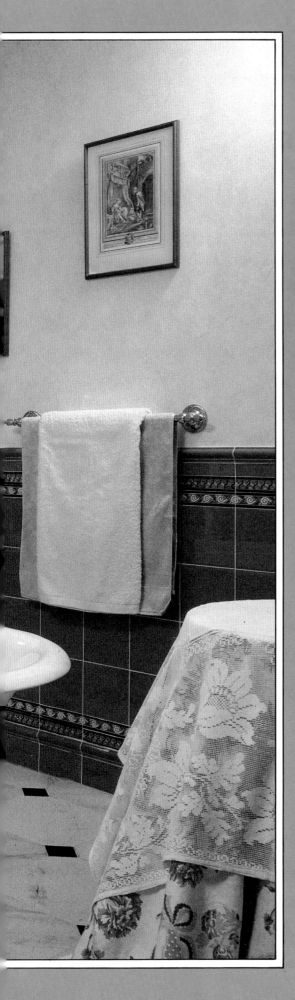

Romantic Interludes

ROMANTIC interiors are everything you've always dreamed of. Infinitely relaxing, with sumptuous seating, feather upholstery, footstools and cushions; invariably nostalgic with scatterings of anniversary flowers (dried and admired), photographs and samplers. Fabrics are light and lacy or heavy and velvety, gathered and draped at windows, around beds and over tables and allowed to tumble in billowing mounds on the floor. Nothing is skimped, pretty cushions are everywhere. Dried or fresh flowers overflow in baskets or jugs. Watercolours or sepia prints decorate the walls and lighting is soft and glowing from a number of lamps rather than spotlights. The romantic interior is derived from the attitude of mind, to be appreciated by both men and women. Giveaway clues are silver cutlery and candles at the dinner table; great bowls of pot pourri and collections of silver photo frames in the living room; lacy cloths and curtains or at least a quilted spread in the bedroom, and in the bathroom mounds of fluffy towels, scented soaps and not a plastic shower curtain in sight. There should be a small corner in every home that's totally frivolous, thoroughly whimsical and yes, romantic, if only to be a place of refuge from the more practical side of home life.

Traditionally romantic bathrooms are created by Pipe Dreams. Here the roll-top bath is positioned in the centre of the room to show off its beautifully patterned exterior. This was stencilled by hand to complement the wall pattern. Naturally even the Victorian-style loo is equipped with modern plumbing.

Burgeoning Romance

The romance of this bedroom lies not only in the relaxing lilac and grey colour scheme, but also in the wonderful view beyond the windows. Here the curtains are never drawn, for as the bed faces the window a romantic scene is set both night and morning. The cushion and lace-strewn sofa add to the romantic nature.

Romance blossomed in this living room at the introduction of the delightful floral painting. From that, the soft peachy colours and the designs on the fabric-painted cushions were taken. The romantic tone is understated but undeniable, creating a wonderfully relaxed atmosphere.

A fresh approach to romance blooms in this bedroom where every edge is softened by pretty fabric, every nook crammed with leafy plants and every surface strewn with all kinds of pottery and lace. The wallpaper and matching curtain fabric set the clear pink and green colour theme here, while the pine washstand and bed lend a traditional air to the room.

Soft Touches

Attic rooms with sloping ceilings and tiny windows still have romantic connotations. The decoration of this living room certainly sets the mood, with its pale colouring, full-skirted table covers and baskets of dried flowers.

The centre of attention in this green and white dining room is the table itself, with its luxurious full-length cloth spilling onto the floor. Co-ordinating curtains edge the window, and by way of contrast are the pretty pieces of pine furniture.

Billowing lengths of fabric are indisputably romantic, for they spell extravagance and luxury. This bedroom has an abundance of both. The bed is surrounded by a canopy and curtains of white muslin, while at the windows the lavish curtains are draped and edged with exotic bows.

Throw Away Lines

Crisp cotton and lace-trimmed sheets, of the kind great-grandma would appreciate, evoke images of lost loves. Smoothed across the end of a bed or draped over a bedside table, they add a touch of romance to many situations.

Casually tossed across a sofa or bed, a travelling rug or shawl can soften any outline and create an intriguingly rumpled effect. For what are romantic notions worth if they don't inject an air of mystery? Soft colours, gentle light and flowers help the illusion.

Opposite: Every bedroom should have an unashamedly feminine alcove, just for sitting and dreaming. Providing the right atmosphere are a lacy shawl, draped over a wicker chair; soft cloths caught in pretty bows and rippling festoon window blinds, all in shades of peaches and cream.

Lacy Looks

Kitchens are rarely thought of as romantic situations but where else would you prepare the food of love? There's just a hint of romance in this pristine kitchen where the frosted windows are edged with lacy scraps and where fresh flowers find a home.

The dressing table is another small area of the bedroom that can be infinitely feminine. Edged with lace, this pine dresser is surrounded by romantic notions: posies of flowers, perfume, a single candle and love birds flying across the wall.

Scraps of lace lovingly gathered at antique markets find a thousand uses for the truly romantic. In this delightful attic bedroom, lace spills across the Victorian fireplace, ripples around cushions and pillows and edges a tiny tray cloth.

Romantic Views

Window treatments can tell a thousand tales, but where romance is concerned the view must be pretty. Here a rather plain window takes on a different guise created by the pine curtain pole which beautifully drapes the broderie anglaise curtains and provides support for the pretty hanging plant.

Modern architecture is no excuse for a lack of romance, especially when with a few metres of lace and ribbon you can achieve delightful settings. Here a lacy pelmet nudges the window, with still more lace loosely wrapped around a pine curtain pole and lavishly caught up with ribbon.

Uninspiring views take on a different outlook when partially covered with disguising café curtains. Here a gilded cage and a variety of plants and flowers attract the attention, while the green and white decoration creates a delightful setting for an intimate meal.

The Classics

EVERY DECADE sees a crop of new, classical furniture, which because of its simplistic design or natural materials remains forever fashionable. Some of the classics from yesteryear – not to be confused with traditional reproductions – are still being made today, possibly because their chrome, leather and steel designs complement the monochrome or bright colour schemes which typify the eighties. Outstanding classics include the chrome and leather Bauhaus chair of the twenties, the rosewood and leather Charles Eammes chair of the fifties and the Plia stacking chair of the sixties. Classics of today which are destined to have that same eternal appeal are the Lizie chair designed by Regis Protiere, and the Strasse dining chair from the Habitat stable. But it's not only furniture that can be counted among the long stayers. Look at lighting: the Art Nouveau Tiffany lamp; the paper shade of the sixties; and today the High-Tech Tizio lamp. Colour, rather than style as such, can also be classic and used fashionably in spite of the decade. Pale green and yellow is classically Georgian, black and white a thing of the fifties and today it's definitely shades of grey with perhaps yellow. Investing in the classics is an investment of a lifetime, like building up a collection of classical music or books, because the designs are so outstanding that their beauty and appeal never fade.

Shades of grey are destined to be synonymous with the eighties, just as pale green was with the Georgian period and shell pink with Rococo. Here too is a blend of classical styles, from the sumptuous drapes to the striking Sheppard Day tiles and Lizie chair.

Mono Tones

Here's a room that spans decades with a variety of classical furnishings. The fireplace is ornate Victorian, the trolley typically Art Deco, while the black Tizio lamp and leather and chrome Medici chairs are very much today's classics. This mixture of styles, in a basically monochrome colour scheme, is also typical of the eighties.

There's nothing self-conscious about this bold scheme that relies as much on its aesthetic linear appeal as on the simplicity of its furniture. The only whimsical touches are the huge plant and the bowl of lemons. But it's the single colour scheme matched with yellow that gives it classical appeal.

Experimentation with colour and design is what new classics are made of, and in the kitchen, such as in this one by Winchmore, it can be as avant garde as the marrying of warm maple wood with a cool, sooty-coloured lacquer.

Classic White

The many shades of white come together in this cool living room, from the creamy white of the leather sofas to the bright white lacquered shelving, and from the misty white of marble to the fresh white flowers. The new classics here are the up-lights and the vases.

The rippling white cupboard doors of these Allmilmö kitchen units will be remembered as one of the innovative classical looks of the eighties. The distinctive contours give light and shade to the white and permit the use of white on walls and floors as well.

Mirror door panels reflect the classic white of gloss paintwork and chequered floor in this dramatic entrance hall. Apart from black, one of the few colours to truly highlight white is red, but it must be used sparingly.

New Colour Combinations

Of all the colours to blend with grey, yellow in all its many shades, from cool primrose to warm melon, is the most important combination. Habitat combine the two colours here in their bedlinen and team them with one of their newest shapes in tubular steel beds.

Mellow yellow makes a sunny impression in a hallway, but contrasting it with mid-grey instead of white creates impact. Lighting is equally as important as colour, with many of the new up-lights, like this Forum metal up-lighter, destined to become classics.

Separately, plain primrose and grey tiles are very dull, but together they are sensational. They're also less expensive than patterned tiles so be lavish with them. In this bathroom tiles are used to create shelves and worktops, and, by keeping the linear design at counter height, create illusions of greater space.

Striking Alternatives

The hard edge of line, and bold colour, creates dramatic impact. Here the classic lines of black and chrome furniture are offset against electric blue and red. But the success of this room relies totally on the predominance of white and grey, on walls and floor, to create the contrast.

The neutral background colour of this living/dining room is in dramatic contrast to the primary colours of the furniture. The lines are strong, the colours bold, but the effect is inviting, helped by the abundance of fresh foliage.

Strong colour is kept at floor level in this bold setting. The rubber stud flooring matched by the blue sofa is contrasted by strong yellow. But, to prevent the whiteness of the walls overpowering the room, the windows have been treated with blue beading.

Soft Options

Canopied beds are a classical look of the past, but this updated version is equally stunning. The generous length of fabric is knotted at the foot of the bed to give a lightness and softness to what was once a heavy effect.

Not all the new classics demand hard edge lines and primary colours. There's still room for softness. The wonderful curves of this new bed shape encourage the use of draped curtains and lacy bedlinen, while the neutral colour theme creates an intriguing impact.

Opposite: No matter what the style of furniture, the softening glow of firelight and candles will convey a classically relaxing atmosphere. Here too the casual throw of a patterned blanket across a plain sofa creates another soft option.

Simplistic Style

THE DESIRE for clutter is polarised between the devotees of Victoriana who wallow in an over-abundance of it, and the followers of John Pawson, who pioneered the minimalist interior. He advocates the barest minimum of furniture, let alone any decorative accessories. Both are design extremes and, although we've come a long way from an excess of possessions, most of us are not quite ready for the minimum. Technology of course is influencing the shift, starting in the kitchen with powerhouses of food processors, microwaves and dishwashers and on to the leisure areas with the compact disc and computer. Architects and designers generally loathe clutter and gradually their ideals are filtering through to us. Furniture is pared down to simple lines, fitted cupboards conceal everything, and even decorative objects like pictures are resting impermanently on the floor instead of the walls. Heavily-patterned fabrics are frowned upon; curtains can be a simple drape of plain muslin across a wooden pole, but Venetian or Roman blinds are preferred; and armchairs are covered with a casual throw, more like a dust sheet, unless they're made of leather. Simplistic interiors such as these require less work and less cleaning; they don't need to be constantly added to or altered, but they do need careful stage-managing initially.

A solitary chaise longue would be praised by the minimalists, but backed by columns of colour and a vase-shaped table light it eludes their dicta. However, it does make an important simplistic statement and proves that, kept to a minimum, 'clutter' can work well.

Single Statement

One beautiful piece of furniture can set the tone for an entire room and demand such attention by its solitary nature as to almost obliterate the presence of anything else. This Le Corbusier chair, though flanked by a chrome table and light, is encouraged to be the dominant feature by the black-framed picture and black and white carpet.

White and green is such a fresh colour combination for a kitchen that it would be a pity to clutter the impression with other colours. The single green chair is the important colour key for the remaining green items in the room.

Although intended for the dining room, the distinctive shape of this black ash chair from Habitat almost demands to stand alone. Displayed against a generous swatch of draped fabric, rather than a conventional curtain, it looks simply stunning.

Mirror Images

A complete wall of mirror such as this effectively doubles the space in a small room. The clever use of horizontal lines allows the eye to travel easily from the real wall to the reflection. For the best effect, however, furnishings must be plain and simple and kept to a minimum.

Simple, low level furniture in this bedroom creates lovely uncluttered images in the mirrored doors of the wardrobes, and allows the unusual wallcovering to make its own positive statement.

Mirror makes it possible to use dark green tiles all over this bathroom, for without its reflection of the white units and light from the window they would have been far too oppressive. A single, off-centre picture is placed for effect, as are the powerful spotlights.

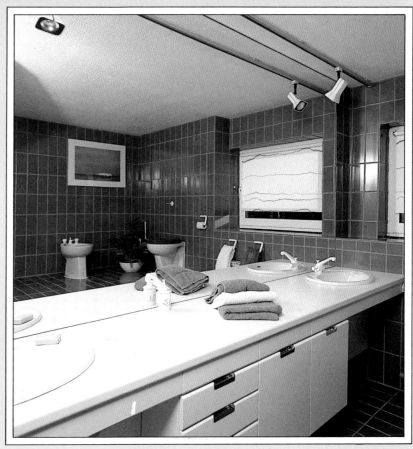

Tri-Colour

It takes courage to stick to just three colours in a room, yet such simplicity can be infinitely more dramatic than a kaleidoscopic scheme. Planned by Dulux, the basis of this scheme is white with simple line form in the Mackintosh-style chair, standard up-light and steel table. By contrast the scattering of red creates a welcome splash of warm colour.

The notion of a four-poster bed gets an updated treatment with a pair of filmy curtains on black poles. Of course they are there just for atmosphere, but the tri-colour theme remains the dominant feature. Again it's centred around the bed with the Dorma linen in red, white and black. Walls fade away in a blur of grey, and furniture is a haze of white.

Opposite: Japanese design is the epitome of simplistic style. The definition of their shapes by black outlines is very important to the look. On the bed, the surprisingly comfortable futon mattress is devoid of cumbersome linen and is central to its unfussy style. So too are the crisp Roman blinds by Sunway, which are neatly striped in the three essential colours.

Light Play

Vertical Venetian blinds are the simplest way to shade long narrow windows, and here the walls and ceiling in a shadow striped paper echo their almost indeterminable filtering of light. Black paintwork outlines the windows and continues the linear effect, at floor and ceiling levels, to the complex shelving unit.

There's a mere hint of curtaining at the windows in this room, since their stripe identically matches those of the wallpaper. The Roman blinds are really there to filter the strong sunlight, while the lightly-covered furniture has a slightly impermanent quality with its dustsheet-style covers.

Opposite: Folding wooden shutters are the traditional filterers of light, and in this almost spartan bathroom they are the true creators of a light pattern on the plain wooden floor, painted walls and white bath.

Pale and Interesting

TIME WAS when 'pale and interesting' meant rather insipid; when 'white' meant white and 'beige' meant porridge-coloured. Today, the notion is really pale but positive. Rainwashed blues and greens, clear peaches and melon yellows. Even white has 'a hint of colour' and beige is definitely muffin-coloured. Paint ranges, especially those created by fabric manufacturers, include many positively pale colours, although it's worth scanning the trade ranges for more interesting shades. Wallpaper manufacturers on the other hand have created just the right pale tones in their sponged, rag-rolled and mosaic-effect papers. One of the most important pale shades is grey, which can be warm or cool depending on the blend of pigments. It's worth considering grey as a basic background shade to any room, especially rooms full of pictures. Misty blue looks marvellous with mahogany furniture while mellow yellow highlights pine. If you're stuck with neutral shades, mix them with pastel colours for an interesting update. Pale patterns are of course important to this positive mix, but this doesn't necessarily mean floral pattern. Consider pale Bauhaus geometrics, shadow soft stripes and neapolitan checks. The choice of accessories can alter the look of a pale room dramatically. Darker shades of the same tone of colour can emphasise a room's softness but too much black or charcoal will bleach away the character. Pale rooms are not as easy to create as you may think, they need careful planning, cross-referencing of colours and blending of soft patterns, but the results are endlessly relaxing, eternally pleasing and unashamedly luxuriant.

Designer Sue Stowell loves subtle, unobtrusive designs and colours with which she likes to achieve a lavish and generous feeling. Her wallpapers and fabrics are used in this beautifully pale bedroom, decorated in shades of soft peach, misty grey and oyster. And consider how stunning they look with the mahogany bedhead.

Preferably Peach

This wonderful kitchen looks almost too good to cook in, decorated as it is in summery shades of pink and mauve. The stencilling is by artists Colleen and Robert Bery, for Dragons, who are specialists in the field of hand-painted furniture, and illustrates the effectiveness of pale colours on tired furniture. The practical note is several coats of lacquer to protect the finish.

Neapolitan shades of peach, green and cream come together in a bathroom which has a movie-star quality with its tiny beaded panels, expanse of mirror and fresh foliage.

Opposite: The restful colours in this peach and grey living room make it a most welcome haven. The cupboards and shelves are painted to blend into the walls, and defining the doors and sofa are thin ribbons of grey to complement the sponge-painted coffee table.

White on White

The pristine whiteness of a kitchen like this may not inspire the best cooking, but it's hard not to appreciate the gleaming cleanness. Interesting softer touches are the faintly-coloured stripes on the tiles and festoon blind.

The white of crisp linen is a luxury that has to be felt to be appreciated. As a bedspread, broderie anglaise is delightful with its delicate eyelet detailing. Here the coolness of white is shaded with a hint of blue and is emphasised by the gleam of old brass.

Opposite: The variety of textures in this tiny rustic living room created so much character that to cover them with colour would have camouflaged their beauty. Creamy white enhances the rough-cast walls, the beamed ceilings and door moulding. Crunchy linen on the sofa blends beautifully, and the rusty brick floor emphasises the combination of white on white.

Misty Tones

Shades of hazy summer mornings colour this restful living room, with its comfortable creamy sofa, soft grey curtains and the understated smattering of sunny yellow.

Delicate rainwashed shades of aqua, mint and hazy blue colour this restful living room, furnished by Next. Here no detail goes unnoticed, from the rippling of the Roman blinds to the camouflaging of the radiators and the matching accessories.

Opposite: Smokey blue is the original colour of this 'Octagon' kitchen by Allmilmö, which teamed with white has the most soothing appearance. Although very modern by design, it has charming traditional features like the porcelain knobs and smooth curved edges to cupboards and counters.

Soft Approach

Coloured bathroom suites can often lose their appeal as fashions change, but this delicate pink suite teamed with apple green tiles has all the eternal freshness of a summer day. The secret of success is the exact continuity of the Dulux paint on the walls and the fake panels.

Resisting the temptation to paint the ceiling in a different colour from the walls and cupboards of this sugar pink room has resulted in a restful atmosphere. This is complemented by a variety of accessories in different colours, but with the same tonal quality of the soft pink. The voile curtains have also been dyed to maintain the continuity.

The walls, floor and ceiling of a study area are coloured in a relaxing sea green, which makes a uniform backdrop for the gleaming white lacquered furniture. A clever choice of picture promotes the colours and provides visual interest.

Neutral Ground

Palest grey, mixed with neutral shades of soft cream, basic beige and hazy yellows, was deliberately chosen to decorate this room so that the tranquil view of the garden beyond the large windows would not be disturbed. Important natural colours of the oak fireplace and the cupboard, reflected in the mirror, together with natural foliage, key the room to the garden outside.

Neutral shades of buff and grey create a placid atmosphere in a dining area. But, far from being cool and characterless, the room responds to the clever use of borders and complementary papers all by Mayfair, which were chosen to enhance the elegant chair and screen.

Mellow yellow is a positive pale that gives character and substance to neutral shades. In this pretty bedroom it emphasises the pine dado rail and bed, without being overpowering, and allows the lacy white duvet and curtains to look fresh and crisp.

Conservatories

PROBABLY the most pleasurable way to extend a house is to add a conservatory. It's a wonderful place to potter if you're mad about plants, a terrific place to relax, especially if it has a sunny south-westerly aspect, and a marvellous addition to the dining room. Practically any glass lean-to can be adapted to the conservatory ideal, but some of the most attractive examples imitate the Victorian styles with their hexagonal shape and pointed roof structure. Apart from good glazing, flooring is a very important feature of a conservatory. Serious gardeners will choose quarry tiles, brick or small flagstones, but as an extension to an internal room use ceramic tiles, vinyl or even wooden floorboards. Wooden staging or rigid shelves, perhaps supported on attractive cast-iron brackets, are important for displaying pot-plants, but purpose-built troughs with good drainage and compost are more valid for the gardeners intending to grow climbers like jasmine or clematis. Vines should really be planted outside the conservatory and then allowed to flourish within its warmth and light. However, too much sunlight can be damaging to some plants, so where there's a southerly aspect blinds should be used to filter the light. Cane and wicker furniture are of course at home in a conservatory and, providing the area is heated to eliminate damp, upholstered furniture can find a home too. Metal tables, converted sewing-machine bases, pine trestles and bamboo tables blend well with the natural foliage, while discreet spotlights, oil lamps and candles create the best lighting.

There's a hint of the Mediterranean in this tall conservatory extension with its arched windows, wooden fan and tropical birds. Mainly for relaxing and entertaining, this room has one window screened with garden trellis and the other shaded with an Austrian blind of Laura Ashley fabric. Palms, ivies and hydrangeas are dotted among the comfortable seating and on the floor are practical quarry tiles.

Sun Traps

A small brick lean-to, with its original stained glass windows and French doors, retains all the character of its Edwardian heritage. White ceramic tiles cover the floor and the brick walls are painted with a 'hint of green' Cover Plus matt vinyl.

Making a wide extension to the living room, this pinnacled conservatory is floored with the same white ceramic tiles for continuity. At the windows are white blinds to control the sunlight and all around the windows is a broad white shelf to hold potted plants. Pine furniture also makes a link with the living room, and for additional comfort there are a couple of slim radiators.

Opposite: Custom-made by Marston and Langinger, this conservatory is based on an authentic nineteenth-century design with its graceful timber-framed windows and filigree metal decoration.

Dining Areas

No more than an ordinary flat-roofed extension, this room has acquired a delightful garden atmosphere with the liberal use of white painted trellis, which is pinned to the walls and ceiling and across the windows. As a heated area it's perfect for lunch or dinner parties or simply for relaxing. On the floor white tiled vinyl is warm and comfortable and pretty curtains in Laura Ashley fabric frame the windows.

Dinner for two, on a warm summer evening, could not be more pleasant than in this tiny conservatory-style extension. Brimming with plants and flowers, the room is lined with green garden trellis, while the wood-board floor is painted dark green to match.

Opposite: The pretty windows of this Edwardian conservatory were marred by the less than attractive sloping glass roof, so white voile was threaded on to curtain wire and stretched across the expanse. This now gives a softer light to what has become a charming breakfast area, overlooked by a fibreglass harlequin.

Indoor Gardens

A galleried living arrangement, with wide skylights overlooking the stairwell, has created a pair of spare areas just perfect for plant life. Light and space create ideal growing conditions and the timbered banisters give a natural surrounding.

A sunny covered courtyard has become a focal point in this timber and brick house. Flanked by the dining room, hall and curved stairway, it has a tiered base of flagstones interspersed by small troughs lined with pebbles. Overhead light encourages tall plants and climbers which are arranged on a variety of stools, tables and shelves.

Opposite: The open-plan masonry construction of this balconied dining area gives all the appearance of the outdoors, especially with the lofty trees growing in the terraced garden. The tiered construction, open walkways and large skylight all add to the illusion of the inside actually being the outside.

Flourishing Rooms

Leading from a converted kitchen, and separated by glass doors, this large conservatory was designed with wide windows to allow maximum light into the kitchen and provide good views of the garden. The white vinyl flooring continues from the kitchen, and because the conservatory is north-facing it did not require sun-blocking blinds. Swedish ivy and variegated hedera frame the kitchen door, while all around, on plant stands and window ledges, are seasonal plants and flowers.

Natural timber forms the basic structure of this wrap-around conservatory, where plant and pond life are equally important. The natural look is extended to the quarry-tiled floor, bamboo blinds and cane furniture, which are in complete harmony with the lush garden beyond.

Opposite: Illustrating how a well-thought-out conservatory can be truly productive, we see in this Marston and Langinger conservatory that vines, palms, oranges and geraniums all flourish well. Wide staging for numerous pot-plants is positioned next to the windows, while a natural flower bed has been dug next to the house wall to encourage climbing jasmine, plumbago and passion flowers. Willow chairs furnish the conservatory and are in complete harmony with the natural foliage.

Kitchens

OF ALL THE rooms in the house, planning a new kitchen deserves the most attention, since it's here that large chunks of the budget will be consumed. Before starting, visit as many showrooms as possible to see just what's available. Make a plan of the positions of units and appliances, choosing an arrangement of work areas to suit your needs. The U-shaped arrangement is the most effective, with the fridge and freezer on one side of the room, sink and dishwasher to one end, and cooker, hotplate and microwave on the other side. Allow plenty of work space in between each area. If there's space, consider a central island area for preparation of meals. Incorporate as many cupboards as you can and don't forget open shelves for decorative storage jars. Think about lighting; you'll need more than one. Under-cupboard lights are useful, but a variety of spotlights over each area can be more effective. Choose your flooring carefully. Ceramic and quarry tiles may fit the character of the room, but vinyl and cork can be more comfortable if you spend a long time in this room. Finally consider the style and colour of your units. White has infinite possibilities to be mixed with contrasting colours; dark colours show up grease and finger marks; while natural wood camouflages grime, but will mellow beautifully with age.

Natural brick and timber are perfect foils for the stained red units in this kitchen. Black-stained timber defines the outline of the cupboards and marries well with the wall-mounted cooker. Powerful down-lights illuminate the work surfaces since natural light is limited, but under-cupboard lights give extra assistance.

Dramatically Different

A blend of the traditional and modern comes together in this kitchen with its white painted brick walls and black laminated units. Since this is actually a very small area, the depth of the work surface is kept to a minimum, permitting only a pair of double burners to be set side by side. Highlighting the area, and creating a greater impression of space, is the projected ceiling, rising to an important skylight.

Architects Bill and Lin Hopper chose a dramatic black and green colour scheme as the basis for their kitchen. The oak-fronted units are arranged in a tight, three-sided plan which allows for a breakfast area as well. Everything was arranged for maximum convenience, with cupboards and appliances packed into a surprisingly small space. A series of down-lights set into the green painted ceiling creates pools of light on the black tiled work surfaces and floor, while the green and black striped blind reflects the overall colour scheme.

Black, red and white is the oustanding colour scheme of this modern kitchen. The walls are lined with oblong, matt white industrial tiles while the oak-fronted units are stained matt black, as are the timber frames of the large picture window. Colour comes from the cherry red flooring and diagonally-striped cherry and white blind.

By Design

Planning a kitchen to fit a large area is, if anything, more difficult than designing a small room. However, many manufacturers, like Moben who designed this kitchen, offer a free planning service to eliminate problems and avoid costly mistakes. This kitchen had an irregular wall which demanded a variety of unit and work surface depths, but it was large enough to accommodate a breakfast bar, which has been cleverly defined by the wooden screen.

Designers Terry and Anne Moore revamped the kitchen of their Victorian home to make it appear lighter and larger. They did this by concentrating the colour on the floor while keeping the walls and units predominantly white. Arranged in a U-shape, the placement of the appliances is classic, with fridge, sink and cooker spaced between ample work surfaces.

Poggenpohl have been designing kitchens for almost a hundred years, and are experts at fitting as much as possible into the smallest space. Here cooker hob, sink and fridge fit neatly into a corner, while open shelves create illusions of space but don't crowd the tiny breakfast bar.

Pretty Traditional

Kitchens never looked quite so pretty before Smallbone introduced hand-painted units. And if you like all those craftsman details edging your shelves, or enclosing your wine-rack, there's plenty of variation to be found in the range. This kitchen goes one step further and highlights the archway between kitchen and breakfast room with trompe l'oeil stonework and vines.

This kitchen was an exercise in ingenuity. Starting life as a plain white room, it was gradually given a traditional character by facing the white cupboard doors with pine and fitting dark blue work tops. A generous mix of plants and old china, together with the Aga cooker, complete the look.

Opposite: Pine will find a natural home in any setting, but it works particularly well in this extended kitchen with its painted brick walls and sunny flower-hung skylight. The true beauty of pine is its ability to blend with any situation and to mellow with time so that eventually new wood looks aged.

Narrow Lines

Creating a large kitchen from a series of small rooms can often result in a number of broken ideas and areas. But in this Victorian house the owners were careful to match up the coving around the room and echo the shape of the new window with that of the arched chimney breast area holding the hob. The central island unit breaks up the long narrow floor space.

It's amazing how much can be tucked into a tiny, narrow kitchen if the space is used effectively. Here cupboards and appliances line up along one wall and are faced with a barrage of cooking utensils hanging from a row of butcher's hooks on metal poles. There's even space for a fold-down breakfast table!

Appliances and cupboards face each other across a narrow kitchen, but the dazzling blind at the far end is so eye-catching that it gives the impression of drawing that wall forward and improving the proportions of the room.

Changing Rooms

Converting a large reception room into a kitchen/dining room can bring some impressive architectural features to the kitchen, which can be accentuated by the choice of units. Here the beautiful mahogany-coloured units of this Moben kitchen complement the Victorian fireplace, stained-glass window and tiled floor to perfection.

There have been no compromises in this kitchen which has been decorated more for the appeal of the area than for the practical side of the room. Grey sponged paper is used throughout with a complementary border at ceiling height. The simple blinds are also grey, as are the trims on the pristine white units. Even the prints in the dining area were chosen to blend with the monochrome scheme.

A country kitchen, in the basement of a town house, reflects the owners' love of good food by positioning the oak dining table right in the middle of the room. The conventional cooker sits neatly within the original fireplace alcove, while the fridge is tucked away behind panelled cupboard doors. A richly-patterned rug on the Suffolk brick floor completes the country look and the warm atmosphere of the room.

Bathrooms

PLANNING a new bathroom from scratch is often easier than trying to adapt the shortcomings of an existing one. Small rooms benefit from the streamlined effect of fitted cupboards and work surfaces, with basin, toilet and bidet built in. If there's not enough space for a full bath, consider a corner bath or simply a shower. Where there's space to spare, build the laundry equipment into a fitted cupboard, or break up the room with a raised dais to create a sunken bath look. New acrylic baths are available in a variety of shapes and colours, and some are even equipped with a whirlpool for a soothing massage. But if you're in any doubt about colour, choose basic white units and bring colour into the rest of the room. For a traditional look in Victorian and Edwardian homes where a bathroom has possibly been created from an extra bedroom, the roll-topped cast-iron baths with heavy claw feet married with reproduction vitreous china basins, loos and high-level pottery cisterns can look completely in character. If it's impossible to replace existing equipment, think about changing the rest of the room with paint and paper. Cover up boring tiles with special tile or deck paint and splash out with an exotic paper for walls, ceiling, doors and bath panels – remember to coat new paper with a sealant if it's not washable. Create interest with mirrors and shelves and scatter fluffy towels and plants about. When there are children in the family choose practical cork or vinyl flooring; otherwise go for the luxury of rubber-backed carpeting. Finally, decorate the window with a pretty blind or panel of stretched lace to complete the new look.

Fitting perfectly into one end of this bathroom, the bath is edged with a deep step and carpeted in exactly the same colour as the suite. The notion of a bath alcove is promoted by the mirror-filled arch and the prettily-draped shower curtain.

New Heights

The impression of a sunken bath can be introduced without altering the floor level of a room, simply by creating a false step beside the bath and covering it with carpet. The architect who designed this bathroom took the procedure one step further by making pine-edged, semi-circular areas beside the bath to hold plants on one side and to contain soiled linen on the other. The pine was continued to define the mirrored arches beside the bath.

This en-suite bathroom is completely colour co-ordinated with the bedroom, and has been given the same luxurious feel. Both areas have beautifully draped curtains and the carpet is extended to surround the bath and cover the fake step. The whimsical notion of a tree beside the bath is created by a painted branch, hung with silk flowers and anchored with Polyfilla into a mirror-edged tub.

Opposite: The sloping proportions of this tiny bathroom lend themselves to the circular bath, which, when surrounded by a tiled ledge and carpeted steps, fitted very neatly into the awkward area.

Reflective Influence

The unconventional bathroom, in a converted Dutch warehouse, backs onto the kitchen from where it has an open-plan view across the living room. The bath and the surrounding wall are all made of pale grey marble slabs. The wall beside the shower is entirely mirrored and adequately reflects the tiny space.

A white vanitory unit with a neat wall of mirrored cupboards above effectively creates a small recess for the toilet which is backed by a trio of decorative glass shelves. Space and light reflected in the mirrors help to make the narrow room look wider.

Infinite reflections are created in this bathroom by placing mirrors on facing walls. To avoid total confusion it's important to keep to a plain colour scheme, with just a plant or picture strategically placed for the most impact.

Inspirational

In keeping with the Victorian style of her home, designer Jean Bird covered one wall of her small bathroom with old tiles, found in junk shops throughout the country. Old pine makes up the vanitory unit and frames the mirror at one end of the room, while antique cotton lace edges the new white blind at the window.

The modern bathroom suite didn't look quite right in this old Sussex house so the owners successfully endeavoured to inject a country atmosphere. The busy wallpaper draws in the walls to give it a cosy feel and pine furniture provides the character.

This exotic bathroom has been lavished with a host of interesting notions to detract from its practical function. Matching curtains edge the window and bath, while the patterned paper over the walls and ceiling complements the café curtains and table cloth. Scraps of lace create a pelmet and top the table, while the patterned vinyl creates a splashback to the lower half of the room.

Panel Games

A charming Edwardian feel is given to this small bathroom with its timbered wall covering and fake panels. It's a richly ambitious scheme which works well because of the reflected light and space in the wall of mirror tiles beside the bath.

Fake panelling achieved with simple beading, on doors, walls and bath panels, creates instant character in bathrooms of any style. Here the pretty trellis wallpaper continued inside the door panels carries through the delicate blue and white colour scheme. Wooden beading edging the vanitory units is a neat finishing touch that's often forgotten.

Opposite: Plain walls take on a totally different character when decorated with beaded panels; they also invite interesting paint effects. Panels on the centrally-located bath are also glossed with Dulux paint to echo the rich colour scheme.

Just Loos

The lack of space in this tiny room is compensated for by the mass of naughty cartoons, memorable photographs and riveting documents, which cover the already highly-patterned walls.

This narrow downstairs toilet has been treated to a fresh green and white colour scheme. Although it contains a variety of patterns, it maintains the same tone throughout. The built-in vanitory unit is edged with tiled shelving, for pretty accessories. Making a divide between the wallpaper and tiles on the wall is broad, white-painted beading.

Opposite: The china toilet bowl, with mahogany seat and surround, plus the wall-mounted cistern, are original fittings which were installed around the turn of the century to a Victorian house in Manchester. In character with the fittings, the room has a plain blue wall covering with blue and beige ceramic floor tiles.

Bedrooms

MORE THAN anything else a bedroom should be restful; a mood that's often created by colour. But colour can tell many different stories. Yellow denotes an optimist; green reflects a need to impress people; brown and neutral shades show a love of the home and family; purple indicates unfulfilment, while red expresses aggression and sensuality. But, whatever colour reflects your personality, aim for co-ordination to maintain a relaxed atmosphere. Beds of course take up most of the space in this room, but their size can be diminished by co-ordinating bedspreads to wallpapers, or exaggerated by an overhanging canopy. Headboards are not essential, but they do seem to make a positive statement even if they are just square cushions suspended from a curtain pole or neatly-gathered fabric stretched between two curtain poles. Brass beds and four-posters are dramatic but they need space to be really effective. Fitted cupboards, papered or painted to match the room, eat up less space than individual wardrobes, and mirrored door fronts can reflect too much clutter in the wrong situation. A dressing table, to be really effective, should be surrounded by plenty of light, either natural or artificial, to prevent unattractive shadows and reflections. Soft lighting is also essential. Overhead lights alone are not enough. Wall lights or individual lamps creating pools of light are more relaxing. And the ultimate luxury, where space permits, is a restful sofa or intimate breakfast area.

Everything in this bedroom is deliberately coloured in neutral tones to create a restful retreat. And, while pattern is liberally used, the designs are soft and swirling. A curvaceous rocker and variety of cushions add to the comfortable quality of the room.

Attic Rooms

Pale blue is one of the most relaxing bedroom colours. In this room the walls and ceiling are painted the same colour and co-ordinate beautifully with a checked fabric. Soft drapes of curtain add to the restful atmosphere, as does the mellow pine furniture and neutral flooring.

High in the roof of an Essex barn, this delightful bedroom has all the elements of a soothing country retreat. Pretty paper covers the walls and ceilings and is matched by the linen; while the variety of pine furniture blends with the rustic character of the room.

Opposite: The sloping walls or ceiling of an attic bedroom can have a soothing, all-enveloping effect on the sleeper, especially if they're decorated in soft and neutral shades. Here the best use of attic space is created by the matching Sanderson wallpaper and fabric and the inclusion of a small writing desk and chair. And, although the bedspread contrasts with the room, the choice of colour blends beautifully.

Well Dressed Beds

The subdued colours which make up the pattern of this quilted bedspread are more than enough to set the warm tone for the rest of the room. Highlighting its pattern is the complementary wallpaper and fabric in golden yellow, emphasised by rich cherry wood furniture.

The oriental influence created by a dramatic bedspread is the keynote to the relaxed atmosphere in this bedroom. The same fabric is interpreted as pictures on the wall, which flank an ingenious, though infinitely soft, bedhead of gathered fabric hung between two curtain poles. The curtains themselves are in the same material and have a matching covered pelmet. Low-level furniture and soft lighting complement this restful setting.

Warm, earth colours are concentrated near the bed, which is surrounded by the natural textures of wood, cane and earthenware, to create a soothing but nevertheless glowing feel in a cool bedroom. And where natural light is pale and cold, pools of warm light can be created with a variety of lamps rather than with a single overhead light.

Sharper Notes

When soft grey is the predominant background colour, primary colours can make a strong statement without creating the jarring notes that cause sleepless nights. Here pale grey coats the walls and floors, while flashes of electric blue and red are concentrated on the bed. The furniture is deliberately simple and stylish to create a sleek contemporary image.

Primary colours surround the bed in this basically white bedroom. Framing the bed are matching curtains held at an angle along the wall by a white curtain pole, while at the window Terylene net curtains are edged with fabric to match. The same patterned fabric also makes up the duvet.

Bright checks of colour pattern the bedspread and window of this boy's room. The interesting bedhead, though primarily a shelving unit, is inset with the same checked fabric and plain red fabric, which is wrapped around foam tubes to create the rippled effect. Red also carpets the floor, while the rest of the room is basically white.

Bright White

Although white, this bedroom takes on a sunny quality created by the yellow carpet. The smattering of sky blue on the American fabric, which patterns the bed and curtains, accentuates the feel. That same fabric has been stiffened and heat-sealed, for extra durability, and used on the cupboard and drawer fronts.

White with a hint of colour creates some of the most restful bedrooms. Here the contrast colour is soft blue, which covers the floor and traces over the bed and wallpaper. The mellow pine furniture blends well with the softness of the scheme, but adding interest is the bright white of the painted brick walls.

Opposite: A pair of nineteenth-century American beds initially had their canopy framework missing, but with expert advice they were recreated and covered with white lace. White also predominates on the bedcovers and walls to maintain the dramatic contrast with the mahogany bed frames.

False Notions

Behind this fake wall, in what is quite a spacious bedroom, is a compact dressing area. The continuation of the turquoise colouring of the walls in both areas strikes a harmonious chord, while the bed remains prettily co-ordinated with the complementary picture above.

The wall between this bedroom and bathroom was only partially removed to create a more spacious feel. Windowless frames on the bedhead wall are fixed with Venetian blinds for discreet separation, though the doorway is left completely open. Co-ordinating colour schemes link the two rooms but practical tiling replaces the more luxurious carpeting on the bathroom floor.

Opposite: Surprisingly there's just one small window in this tiny bedroom. The frames above the bed are actually fake, but have been inset with matching roller blinds to create the illusion of more windows. However, the pale colour scheme of apricot and lilac ensures a feeling of spaciousness which is dramatised by the angle-poise lamps.

Dining Rooms

TODAY THE true dining room is an enigma. Once the bastion of good manners, it has become the family room, study or sewing room as well. Choice of adaptable furniture is therefore essential: perhaps fitted cupboards with a solid, pull-out work surface or desk; fold-up chairs; or an extending or folding table, which will be inconspicuous most of the time, but which can be enlarged to accommodate more people on special occasions. A small square or round table, used for family meals, can be enlarged with a circle of chipboard cut to the required size, then positioned on the table and draped with a full-length cloth. A traditional sideboard is of little use in a multi-purpose room, but could be replaced by a flat-topped desk or dresser, which could be used for serving food as well as for a working or storage area. Lighting, as always, is important. Consider an adjustable light positioned over the dining table with spotlights or lamps over working areas. Candlelight for special dinners is very flattering but should be kept to a height above or below eye level, and should be teamed with soft lighting elsewhere in the room. Carpets in the dining room must be stain-resistant if they're to keep their good looks. Alternatively consider wooden flooring in ash or oak which blends with any style of furniture. Cork or vinyl tiles are also practical where animals and young children are part of the family. At the window Venetian blinds or wood slat blinds look attractive, for, although curtains may have a softer look, fabrics do absorb smells, so always choose easily-washable materials.

None but the orderly cook can cope with the kitchen diner arrangement. Here smart painted cupboards hide the clutter while open shelves and butcher's hooks hold much-used equipment. The floor and work surfaces are covered with easily-maintained tiles. Plain windows, good lighting and a stunning, yet plastic-coated table cloth cope with the practicalities of cooking and eating together.

Flexible Rooms

When the living and dining areas are in the same room there can be certain design problems of equating functional dining furniture with relaxing sofas and cushions. Here the problem has been resolved by using a prettily-shaped table which has been splatter-painted to complement the overall decoration of the room.

Open-plan living creates its own ground rules in choice of furniture and lack of clutter. Everything, whether decorative or functional, must have a purpose and a place. In this Dutch flat, the small kitchen area is divided from the dining room by a marble-topped counter, while all the visible equipment is neatly arranged. Though small, the dining table will actually seat six and the pine dresser stores the china. The baby grand may be large but it is a focal point and display area.

Opposite: This living and dining room had its areas neatly separated by the low wrought-iron balustrade. Although a narrow area, the clever use of pine benches and single pews creates seating for eight around the table. Glass display shelving and attractive hanging lights add to the feeling of space.

Floor Level

Quarry tiles are a positive asset in this narrow dining room which has patio doors to the garden at one end, and backs onto the kitchen at the other. The colour is perfect for the situation where even muddy footprints can be cleaned away easily.

Combined with the hall this modern dining room looks perfectly at home with the practical grey vinyl floor tiles. It's a colour that blends with the decoration and a style that complements the chrome, glass and white painted furniture.

Opposite: Although traditionally furnished with mahogany and pine, this dining room is mindful of the practicality of vinyl flooring. In a neutral shade it blends into the background of the room and allows the more interesting elements to stand out.

Window Treatments

Shocking pink Pleatex blinds look stunning in this cool, pale grey dining room. Made of strong, permanently pleated paper, they can be made to fit any window and look similar to Venetian blinds when in use, but cost half the price.

French doors opening onto a sunny patio from the dining room require nothing more than plain white roller blinds to filter the sunlight and complement the fresh green and white colour scheme. White curtains could have been used but they would have seemed fussy in this situation and could have blocked not only the light but the view as well.

Opposite: The window treatment in a pretty cottage dining room can be as frivolous as you like. Here the outer curtains, in one pattern, are matched by the frilled pelmet and wallpaper, while the inner curtains, which are drawn at night, are in a plainer complementary fabric.

Traditional Looks

In character with the atmosphere of this Yorkshire farm house, the dining room furniture is rustic, though high-polished, oak. Rich, red fabric curtains the windows and covers the seat cushions, while traditional brass and china fittings are all around.

Elegant dining with mahogany furniture, bone china and family portraits is only a nod away from the functional kitchen. The draped curtains, though open at the start of the meal, are easily closed to enhance the candlelit atmosphere throughout the dinner.

Warm peach and mahogany complement each other perfectly in this traditional dining room, where even the sofa, used for relaxing after the meal, is covered in the same shade. At the shuttered windows both curtains and festoon blinds are used, but only the blinds are closed at night.

Individual Rooms

Geometry plays an important part in this highly individualistic room, but space and colour are the key elements making the choice of pattern really work. The black lacquer table and chairs relate directly to the floor, while the straight lines of the wallpaper reflect the patio doors and bookcase.

To bring a little of the garden inside was one of the criteria when building this Worcestershire home. And in no room is it more evident than in the dining area. Here creamy pink facing bricks are the main element, used on the walls and central planter, where weeping fig plants (grown by the hydroculture method, in pebbles instead of soil) soar up to the high glass roof. A series of down-lighters illuminates the rest of the room.

There can be nothing more welcoming in the hallway of a large house than beautiful wood furniture and a friendly fireplace. This hall contains both and doubles as an elegant dining room, where against a background of ivory paintwork and a white ceramic-tiled floor the furniture looks very rich.

Living Rooms

FURNISHING and decorating a living room requires more than a touch of realism. First of all consider the use of the room. Will it be more of an action room where the children will play, have parties and watch television? Or will it be an adults-only room for relaxing, entertaining or listening to music? Practically speaking, good-quality carpeting is essential, but wood-block flooring, coir matting or cork are more robust, and can look very stylish topped with the right rugs. The choice and style of furniture depend on the budget, but an initial investment in a good sofa and a matching chair, with loose covers in a tough fabric, is a good basis. However second-hand antique furniture covered in smart fabric might well be more suitable. Unit seating can be bulky but useful in a family with young children. Adequate storage for books, music equipment and the television is also important – try to conceal all those wires! Shelving built into an alcove or incorporated within a system looks more attractive than spaced individually around the room and can involve interesting lighting. Generally, lighting should be a mixture of overhead lamps, perhaps controlled by a dimmer switch, plus secondary lighting from table lamps for atmosphere. Colour schemes, of course, are a matter of individual choice but a neutral background colour in grey, cream or white allows plenty of scope for additional colour within the room. Rich pattern, especially on seating, is practical and full of character, but softer patterns and colours are more relaxing.

Neutral colours were used for the floor, walls and furniture in this narrow living room to allow the superb lacquered piano to take pride of place. Note the attractive trellis work which encloses an old-fashioned radiator.

Comfortably Traditional

The drawing room of a Berkshire home has all the elements of a stylish family room. Here cream-coloured walls and curtains provide a neutral background to the richly-patterned overlay of rugs, red lacquered table and patterned sofas. In the corners, two colourful tables with floor-length cloths are scattered with family treasures, while the marble fireplace is surrounded by mirrors to reflect the scene.

Cream walls and flooring are the natural colour elements of this drawing room, but strong colour on the sofas and at the window balances the large wall-hanging which is the room's focal point.

Peach and grey is the colour theme for this elegant drawing room which leads an orderly life without children. Matching sofas face each other across a low coffee table, with a single Victorian chair for additional seating. Interestingly the view of the busy London street beyond the window is screened by attractive white panelling instead of net curtains.

Mood Lighting

The living room of a small modern flat makes up for the minimal furniture by the use of good colours, simple furniture shapes and moody lighting. On the walls, chrome lamps throw a soft light around the room, while a stronger light is concentrated on the table. Flickering background light is decoratively arranged by a tray of candles.

Richly-patterned fabric can create a distinctive mood in a living room. Here the swirling design on the sofa is complemented by striped curtains and wallpaper. Everything else is very plain. Adding to the mood is a glass vase light, which creates a soft up-lit glow to the edge of the room.

Strong colours set against natural walls and flooring in a very uncluttered setting are the basis of this living room, where modern and traditional furniture live in harmony. It's an adult room designed for conversation rather than play, with just one beautiful accessory in the shape of the glowing Art Deco lamp.

Shelf Evident

In a busy living room like this, storage is important. It's found under the seat in the window for magazines and games, within the cupboards for stereo equipment and inside the drawers for tapes, writing paper and general clutter. The display shelves and the console table keep all the decorative pieces neatly along one wall.

Two shades of blue Cover Plus paint colour this elegant living room. The cleverly incorporated shelving echoes the colours and provides high-level storage for books, but there's an important low-level shelf for the television and stereo, which conceals unsightly wiring and plugs under its flip-top lid.

Though tiny, this living room is perfectly furnished for a young couple. A warm background colour has toning plain and patterned furniture, while the neat but very important shelving is provided by a free-standing cabinet with roller shutters.

Richly Coloured

Vivid pink curtains are a bold statement in any room, but particularly in the living room where relaxation is the keynote. Here they are married with soft peach walls and a richly-patterned rug so their presence is not overpowering. Neutral flooring and furnishings are essential to the scheme.

Bold stripes on both the rug and the curtains in this living room have a dramatically rich quality when all else is plain. Left in its calico cover, the sofa will eventually pick up one of the three curtain shades to anchor the colour at this end of the room. Natural wood-block flooring and neutral paintwork, however, complement the sofa in its present state.

Scarlet is stunning, of course, and not nearly as difficult to live with as you may think. It's such a clear colour, which, when offset against ivory-coloured paintwork and flooring, then contrasted with black furniture and dark green plants, creates a positive yet nevertheless comfortable setting.

Natural Influence

The beauty of natural colours is their ability to complement any style of furnishing. Here the atmosphere is distinctly eastern with the beautiful ratan furniture, wood slat blinds and wall-hung dhurries. Of course it's important to be completely neutral, to maintain the soothing atmosphere, which would be broken with the introduction of any primary colours.

Classically elegant rooms, rich with mahogany wood and oil paintings, require a great deal of restraint to remain neutral. Here the walls are cream, matched by calico festoon blinds and furniture. The floor is sisal which adds a deeper natural tone. By way of contrast, but still quite neutral, are the stone lions supporting the glass table top.

Opposite: The rustic, though importantly architectural, quality of this room, with its soaring brick chimney and rising beams, required neutral yet warm furnishings to complement its form.

Children's Rooms

BY NATURE most children are untidy – neatness is a skill that's hopefully acquired by adults. Storage is therefore very important in a child's room so he or she can learn at an early age to put things away. A wardrobe with perhaps a two-tier system of rails to maximise the space and make some clothes easy to reach. A toy box or cupboard fitted with wire or plastic trays to separate trains from robots and dolls from dressing-up clothes. A proper work station to encourage an area for drawing and writing and eventually homework. Easy linen, like fitted sheets and duvets, means that bed-making is easy for you and them. Blinds instead of curtains for the same reason. A good reading light for bedtime is important and perhaps a table lamp for a night light. Washable paper or vinyl paint is a must, and practical cork, vinyl or cord flooring, for obvious reasons. Naturally children prefer primary colours, but avoid busy wallpapers in preference for plain walls with coloured paintwork and linen – their appeal will last much longer. A large pinboard also encourages a respect for good decoration while not restraining the child's instinct to display his or her own work.

A high-level bunk bed reached by a rope ladder allows plenty of room for storage, plus display and work area below. Practical vinyl flooring, in white and yellow, sets the colour theme for the cupboard door edges, handles and accessories. Good spot lights illuminate the desk and bunk bed.

Working Bunks

Converted lofts make marvellous children's rooms, providing ample space for bunk beds, a desk, storage and a play area. Here the practical wood flooring matches the roof structure, which is also hung with spotlights. The bunk beds have colourful covers and scatter cushions creating daytime seating (duvets come out at night), while the wide table alongside is a good work station.

Work and storage areas created around and under the bunk beds make the best use of the elevated arrangement. This purpose-built bunk is fitted with wire baskets under the bed, like the ones found in wardrobes. A bracketed shelving system is clipped to the bed frame and includes the desk. The striped wallpaper and bedcover are matched by a red edging to the shelves and storage area.

Opposite: A perfect working and sleeping arrangement is provided in this narrow box room. Important points are the bunk's safety rail, Venetian blind at the window and wide play-cum-study bench below the bunk, which if adequately supported could also be used for a second bed when friends come to stay.

Young Ones

Delightful nurseries are irresistible, but long-term planning can make them adaptable as well. Chosen to grow up with the child, this wallpaper looks lovely with the frilled crib. Later curtains, blind and plain white fittings will delight any little girl. Dispense with the curtains and keep the red blind and it's perfect for a boy.

Small babies are stimulated by bright colours and moving objects, all of which are provided in this nursery. Interesting additions are the painted clouds on the ceiling, the neatly frilled pelmet around the awkward window and the use of the colourful border.

Clever play areas for slightly older children can be created with a painted screen. Made from blockboard with window and door shapes cut out, this screen is a make-believe house, but the same principle could create a train, boat or space ship.

Girls' Rooms

A seventeenth-century four-poster bed was the basis for this lovely room, with the drapes around the bed matching those at the window. The same effect could be created around an ordinary divan by draping curtains from a 45-cm semi-circle of blockboard bracketed to the wall above the bed. Curtains could be stapled to the rim of the blockboard then covered at the join with a pelmet of fabric.

An ordinary bunk bed acquires the appeal of a four-poster by hanging curtains around the bottom bunk. The supporting curtain wire is covered by a frilled pelmet which is joined to the bunk with Velcro. Matching duvet covers and a pretty blind complete the picture.

For a young teenager more dedicated to pen friends and ponies, a more orderly room is preferable. Practical shelves and desk are fitted to the base of this bunk and just a hint of feminity is created by the draped curtain.

Boys' Rooms

Ensuring the long-term future of this boy's room, the duvet and blind are in a tough striped fabric, and on the blind is a simple yet very effective applique. The wicker hamper makes a good storage basket for toys, as do log baskets, old ship's trunks and blanket boxes.

Not quite so ambitious, this boy's room features an old wardrobe painted and patterned, and fitted with two pole handles. The walls, which are plain white, are reserved for cut-outs and mobiles and on the top bunk there's a shiny plastic cover creating a play area.

Opposite: Creating an all-enveloping mural like this is a professional job, but a novice could create similar effects by painting the room dark blue, then shading in lighter blue and grey around pictures cut from posters. Lighting is important for effect. Here there's an oval bulkhead ceiling light and a spotlight on the facing wall.

Teenage Rooms

A keen eye for detail and a steady hand take this room in the right direction. Colour-striped Venetian blinds are the keynote with their colours extended onto the wall, over the beds then onto the floor with lino paint.

Decorated with conviction, the walls and ceiling of this teenager's room are painted with vinyl, the floor with deck paint. Important natural light is available from two areas, both covered with Venetian blinds, one cunningly painted. Simple metal furniture is kept to a minimum, with comfortable seating provided by a deck chair.

Opposite: Study areas within a bedroom make sense for teenagers and adults alike, and tucked into an alcove they can be as obtrusive or discreet as you want. Painted in primary Cover Plus paints this area is well organised with space for filing, a wall grid for additional storage and good concealed lighting over the work area.

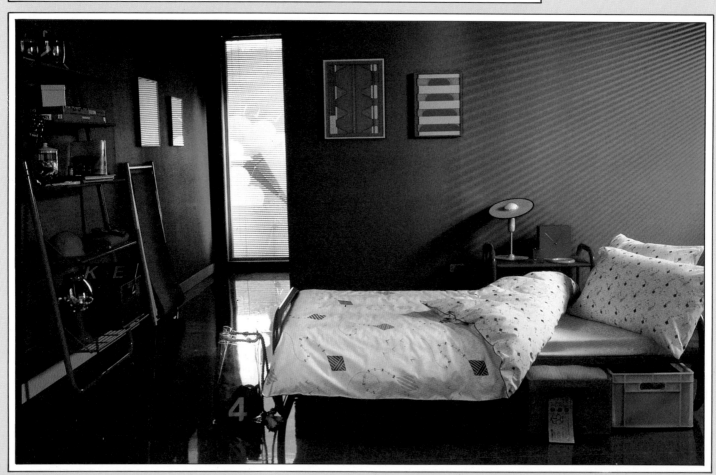

Hallways

AS THE introduction to a home, the hall should create the right first impression. Decorate small areas with a dramatic colour scheme to detract from their lack of size. Add new dimensions with long mirrors or paint the ceiling with white gloss to reflect light and space. Break up an expanse of wall in a narrow hall with a built-in unit to enclose a radiator, create a hall table or provide a display area. If this takes up too much room, place a dramatic painting or poster on the wall facing the door to catch the eye and diminish the corridor feel. An attractive table and chair always look inviting in a larger hall, with perhaps some discreet shelving around the front door, or a theatrical swag of fabric to separate the clutter of prams, bicycles and wellies from the telephone table. Flooring of course must be heavy-duty Wilton. Highly-patterned Axminster could be overpowering and clash with adjacent rooms. Alternatively use robust cord or sisal. Marble tiles and some of the new vinyl tiles can look very elegant, while quarry tiles and polished floorboards have a country feel. Lighting can be tricky but it might be worth considering a series of down-lights to illuminate a dark hall, or additional power points to accommodate small lamps and picture lights in larger areas. But, if you're stuck with just one ceiling light, make it as interesting and attractive as possible.

Some pre-war homes have solid panels instead of balusters surrounding the staircase, which can be less attractive and block out light. New balusters and handrails are pricey but could be worth the investment on a dark landing.

On the Rails

This stunning spiral staircase with its mahogany handrail is an original feature of a Georgian home. Happily the plain walls, smooth alcove and straight balusters are simple enough not to detract from its shape.

The wooden staircase in this traditional cottage was practical, though a little out of character. Plants and an antique high-backed chair soften its outline, while interesting portraits attract attention to the beamed wall behind.

Opposite: The balusters in an Edwardian house were beautifully shaped, but badly chipped and dented, so the owners painted them white, but made a feature of the handrail by marbling it in shades of ochre, cream and brown. Two coats of lacquer ensured a tough, shiny surface.

Completely Floored

Stripped floorboards, waxed and polished to a mellow hue, could be all that a hallway needs to give it character. Interestingly these floorboards span the hall giving it a much wider appearance. A rug would be an unnecessary addition to this hall, but if one were used it should always have a non-slip backing.

The vestibule of this converted country chapel is floored with burnished brick, which leads into the living area. The polished mahogany console table indicates the character of the room beyond, while beautiful pale light streams in through the arched window above the heavy oak doors.

The intriguing combination of colours on these Sheppard Day linoleum tiles gives it a three-dimensional effect which is infinitely striking. Based on eighteenth-century marble tiles, they definitely look at home with traditional furniture and give a completely new meaning to lino.

Stunning Staircases

Although long and narrow, this hallway in an Edwardian house takes on new dimensions within the vast expanse of mirror. Rising up the staircase, carefully-arranged pictures cover the wall and draw attention to the stencilled border and ceiling details.

Raspberry pink is not the first colour you'd think of for a hallway, but having designed his Regency Stripe wallpaper, which is used on the walls, designer Christian Hills knew it would bring warmth and interest to this stunning hallway.

There's definitely an air of the Art Deco era about this hallway, with its shaped stairway and bank of theatrical lights. White, defined by natural wood, creates a dramatic effect, but the soft grey carpet adds a touch of luxury.

Inner Space

In a modern home where the front door opens right onto the dining alcove and adjacent living room, it's important to keep the areas co-ordinated. Here there are black tiles on the floor and smart shadow striped paper on the walls. The grey hall table doubles as a desk and matches the dining table, while the living room sofa picks up all the colours.

The hallway to the side of this house aims to bring much of the garden greenery inside. The vinyl flooring also has a terrazzo feeling, as does the effective garden urn.

Opposite: Careful planning was essential to the design of this hallway. Vital floor space was sacrificed to house deep cupboards, which created a bedroom platform above. But there's enough space at ground level for a neat roll-top desk and adjacent bookshelf. The prolific plant marries the two areas and draws attention to the important skylight.

Dramatic Entrances

A variety of timber effects create this dramatic red and black entrance hall. Wooden doors and plain walls are painted glossy red but the horizontal wood cladding contrasts in a blue black stain. The grey carpet running throughout the area and into the living room combines the two colours. Natural wood frames the doorways and cleverly-constructed alcoves.

Fair-faced bricks line the floor and walls in this hallway, which has been cleverly lit by a series of bright spotlights to accentuate their colour and texture. The whole area is consciously free of clutter and furniture which would simply detract from the powerful impact of the brick.

Opposite: The converging lines of beams, balconies and windows create a wonderful aspect from the wide hallway below. Natural materials of timber, quarry tiles and foliage look particularly dramatic against the plain white walls.

PICTURE CREDITS

The author and publishers would like to thank the following companies for supplying additional photographs.

Country House: page 18 – Dorma; page 20 – Sanderson, page 21 – Terylene (DG404) John Aird; page 25 – Dulux; page 26 – Smallbone of Devizes.
City Looks: page 31 – Laura Ashley; page 35 – Dorma.
Special Effects: page 39 – Interior Selection; page 40 – (5489) Stiebel; page 40 – Cover Plus; page 41 – Smallbone of Devizes, Collier Campbell, Dragons of Walton Street; page 42 – Peter Payne; page 43 – Tim Plant; page 44 – Dulux.
Colour Confidence: page 48 – Cover Plus; page 49 – Laura Ashley; page 53 – Cover Plus.
Designer Touches: page 58 – Sue Stowell; page 58 – Smallbone of Devizes; page 60 – Smallbone of Devizes; page 60 – Collier Campbell; page 61 – Poggenpohl; page 63 – Next.
Inspirational: page 67 – Runtalrad Ltd; page 70 – Collier Campbell, Dorma.
Romantic Interludes: page 82 – Pipe Dreams; page 87 – Sunway Blinds; page 88 – Dulux.
The Classics: page 90 – Sheppard Day Designs;

page 92 – Winchmore; page 93 – Allmilmö; page 94 – Habitat.
Simplistic Style: page 100 – Habitat; page 102 – Dulux, Dorma; page 103 – Sunway Blinds.
Pale and Interesting: page 106 – Sue Stowell; page 108 – Dragons of Walton Street; page 112 – Next, Allmilmö; page 114 – Dulux; page 115 – House of MayFair.
Conservatories: page 116 – Laura Ashley; page 119 – Marston and Langinger Conservatories; page 118 – Cover Plus; page 120 – Laura Ashley, Dorma; page 125 – Marston and Langinger Conservatories.
Kitchens: page 129 – Moben Continental Kitchens Ltd, Poggenpohl; page 130 – Smallbone of Devizes; page 133 – Moben Continental Kitchens Ltd.
Bathrooms: page 141 – Dulux.
Bedrooms: page 147 – Sanderson; page 149 – (St Tropez) Tyrone Textiles, Terylene.
Living Rooms: page 168 – Cover Plus; page 170 – Cover Plus.
Children's Rooms: page 175 – Dulux; page 181 – Cover Plus.
Hallways: page 186 – Sheppard Day Designs.